CULTURES OF THE WORLD

Panama

Cavendish
Square

New York

Published in 2017 by Cavendish Square Publishing, LLC
243 5th Avenue, Suite 136, New York, NY 10016
Copyright © 2017 by Cavendish Square Publishing, LLC

Third Edition

Library of Congress Cataloging-in-Publication Data

Names: Hassig, Susan M., 1969- | Quek, Lynette. | Nevins, Debbie.
Title: Panama / Susan Hassig, Lynette Quek, Debbie Nevins.
Description: Third edition. | New York : Cavendish Square Publishing, [2017] |
Series: Cultures of the world | Includes bibliographical references and index.
Identifiers: LCCN 2016036878 (print) | LCCN 2016037078 (ebook) | ISBN 9781502622150 (library bound) | ISBN 9781502622167 (E-book)
Subjects: LCSH: Panama--Juvenile literature.
Classification: LCC F1563.2 .H38 2017 (print) | LCC F1563.2 (ebook) | DDC 972.87--dc23
LC record available at https://lccn.loc.gov/2016036878

Writers: Susan Hassig, Lynette Quek; Debbie Nevins, third edition
Editorial Director, third edition: David McNamara
Editor, third edition: Debbie Nevins
Associate Art Director, third edition: Amy Greenan
Designer, third edition: Jessica Nevins
Production Coordinator, third edition: Karol Szymczuk
Cover Picture Researcher: Angela Siegel
Picture Researcher, third edition: Jessica Nevins

PRECEDING PAGE
Entrance to the Panama canal, as seen by air

Printed in the United States of America

CONTENTS

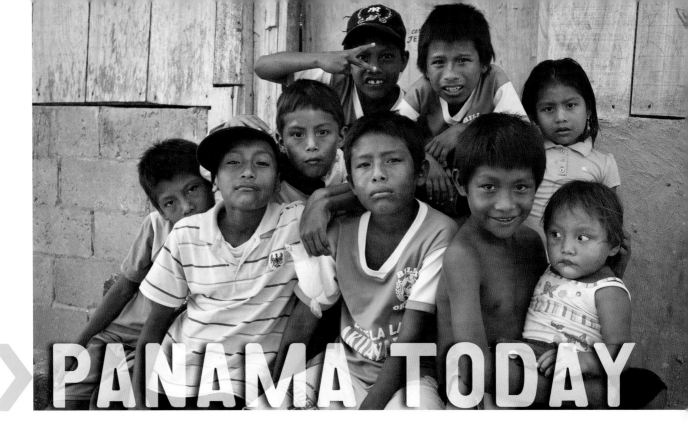

PANAMA TODAY

ON AUGUST 12, 2014, AN UNUSUAL BUILDING OPENED IN PANAMA City, the capital of Panama. Designed by one of the world's most famous architects, the Canadian-American Frank Gehry, whose wife is Panamanian, the fantastical new structure debuted to public expressions of both wonder and scorn—as Gehry's works often do. Looking more like a tumbling pile of toys than a natural history museum, the whimsical Biomuseo has an awesome mission. "The building was designed," its website says, "to tell the story of how the Isthmus of Panama rose from the sea, uniting two continents, separating a vast ocean in two, and changing the planet's biodiversity forever." The Biomuseo is Gehry's only work in Latin America and the tropics.

Sitting near the entrance to the Panama Canal on the Pacific Ocean side, the museum is a monument to the country's extraordinary place in the natural world. The Isthmus of Panama is a narrow land bridge connecting the continents of North America and South America. Technically, it is the southernmost extension of North America, but Panama is more often thought of as one of the seven countries of Central America. Its geographic distinctiveness and biodiversity are the museum's

The fanciful Biomuseo in Panama City has eight galleries dedicated to Panama's natural history and biodiversity.

themes. However, with its eye-popping colors and futuristic configurations, the building itself is a vibrant symbol of Panama's improving economic and political status and its goal of becoming a world-class beacon for the Americas.

In the twenty-first century, things have been going quite well for Panama. Indeed, in 2015, for a second year in a row, the Gallup-Healthways Global Well-Being Index named Panama the happiest place on earth. That is, the organization's annual survey found Panamanians to have the world's highest rating for overall well-being, according to certain self-reported criteria. Out of the 145 countries surveyed in 2014, Panamanians scored the highest overall, with 53 percent of them said to be "thriving" in three or more of the following five categories:

PURPOSE: liking what they do each day and being motivated to achieve their goals,

SOCIAL: having supportive relationships and love in their lives,

FINANCIAL: managing their economic lives to reduce stress and increase security,

COMMUNITY: liking where they live, feeling safe, and having pride in their communities, and

PHYSICAL: having good health and enough energy to get things done daily.

A Native woman and her daughter are among the indigenous people who keep Native cultures alive in Panama.

The report found that Latin Americans in particular have higher levels of well-being than any other regional group: "Residents of many Latin American countries are among the most likely in the world to report daily positive experiences such as smiling and laughing, feeling enjoyment, and feeling treated with respect each day." In addition to that cultural predisposition, the report said other factors contributing to Panama's top score might include its "relative political stability, a strong and growing economy in 2014, and investments in national development." (For comparison, the United States that year came in at number 23.)

To be sure, such concepts as happiness and well-being are hard to quantify with numbers. Other surveys measuring global well-being use different criteria, and therefore arrive at different conclusions. The UN's World Happiness Report for the same period crunched the numbers using indicators such as gross domestic product (GDP) and life expectancy figures, along with more elusive variables. It named Denmark number 1 out of 157 nations, while Panama scored a 25.

Thirty years ago, Panama wouldn't have attained a good rating in any such survey. The country endured decades of military dictatorship marked by corruption and human rights violations. Today, Panama is still emerging from those troublesome years, and some of the problems rooted in that era continue to challenge the country's progress.

When President Juan Carlos Varela took office in 2014, surveys revealed that the public's top concerns were poor water supplies for some rural segments of the population, electricity shortages, and dismal conditions in public schools. Corruption remains a concern. The previous president Ricardo Martinelli, his son, and various other officials have been implicated in a number of corruption scandals. Corruption is reportedly widespread in the government's judicial branch as well.

Panama's banking and financial service industry is one of its most robust economic sectors. However, it has long had a reputation as a haven for illicit money—that is, as a safe place for wealthy people and public officials to stash ill-begotten funds, effectively shielding the dirty money from prying eyes. Recently, Panama's government has tried to clean up its reputation by passing stricter anti—money laundering laws. However, the unsavory side of the business was revealed in a harsh light in April 2016 when 11.5 million private documents were leaked to the media in a scandal dubbed "The Panama Papers." The records of the Panamanian firm Mossack Fonseca document the fraud, tax evasion, and other illegal practices of its extremely wealthy international clients, many of whom are well-known people. The country of Panama itself was not the focus of the investigation—but the unpleasant mess cast a shadow over it nonetheless.

On a much more positive note is the recent expansion of the Panama Canal. Undoubtedly Panama's most famous asset, the 48-mile (77-kilometer) artificial waterway bisects the country, creating a long-dreamed-of maritime shortcut between the Atlantic and Pacific Oceans. Since its opening in 1914, the canal had belonged to the United States, the country that built it. In 1999, the United States handed over full ownership of the canal and its properties to Panama. That momentous event essentially granted Panama the full independence and national coherence it had lacked under US domination throughout most of the twentieth century.

Panama got right to work widening and deepening the canal, which had become somewhat obsolete due to the bigger dimensions of today's mega-sized tanker ships. The $5 billion expansion project, started in 2007, finally opened in 2016 to great celebration. The canal project has already boosted

Panama's economy, creating thousands of new jobs and stimulating other construction and growth in both Colón and Panama City, the Atlantic and Pacific entryways to the canal. While Panama certainly has many problems yet to solve, recent progress has been promising. Because of its unique location, this country of gleaming cities and dense rain forests has long been called "the bridge to the world." Today that may be truer than ever before.

This 2016 aerial view shows the Gatún Locks section of the newly completed Panama Canal expansion.

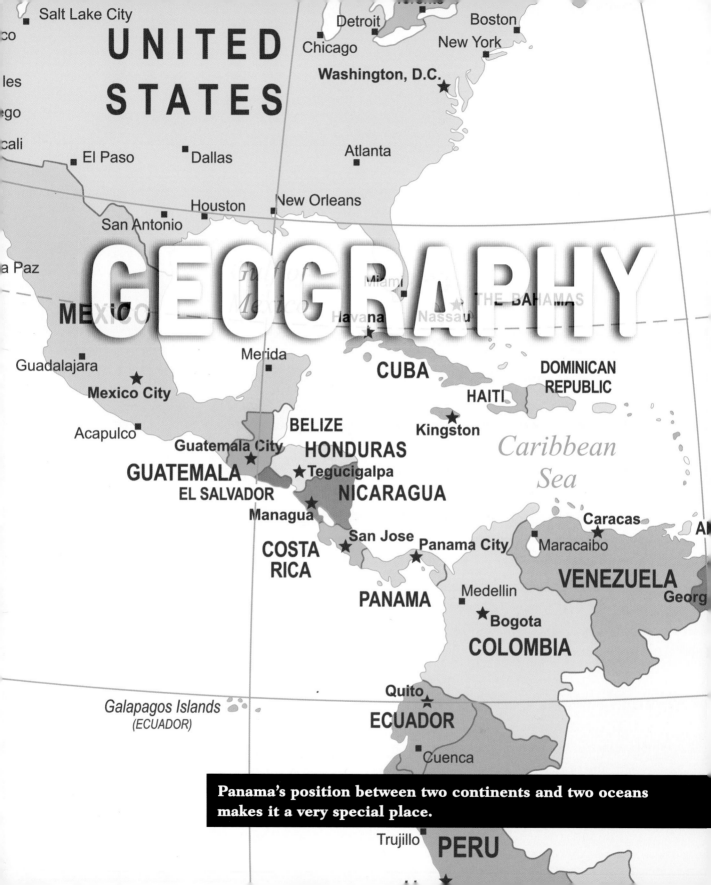

Salt Lake City

UNITED
STATES

Detroit
Chicago

Boston
New York

Washington, D.C.

El Paso · Dallas

Atlanta

Houston
San Antonio

New Orleans

a Paz

GEOGRAPHY

Miami

THE BAHAMAS

MEXICO

Gulf of Mexico

Havana

Nassau

Guadalajara

Merida

CUBA

DOMINICAN
REPUBLIC

Mexico City

HAITI

Acapulco

Kingston

Caribbean
Sea

Guatemala City

BELIZE
HONDURAS

GUATEMALA
EL SALVADOR

Tegucigalpa

NICARAGUA

Managua

Caracas

San Jose

Panama City

Maracaibo

COSTA
RICA

Medellin

VENEZUELA

PANAMA

Georg

Bogota

COLOMBIA

Galapagos Islands
(ECUADOR)

Quito

ECUADOR

Cuenca

**Panama's position between two continents and two oceans
makes it a very special place.**

Trujillo PERU

1

P ANAMA IS A FAIRLY SMALL COUNTRY in the Central American part of North America, but it is located in a very strategic place. Panama covers 29,120 square miles (75,420 square kilometers), which is slightly smaller in area than the state of South Carolina. Panama sits on a narrow strip of land called an isthmus, between the world's largest bodies of water, the Atlantic and Pacific Oceans. This loosely S-shaped country connects the North and South American continents, bordering Costa Rica to the west and Colombia to the southeast.

Because of Panama's unusual shape and location, some parts of the country see the sun rise over the Pacific Ocean and set over the Atlantic Ocean.

Panama's geographic and historic importance is highlighted by the fact that it has five World Heritage Sites. These exceptional cultural and natural places have been deemed by the United Nations Educational, Scientific and Cultural Organization (UNESCO) to be of "outstanding value to humanity" and therefore worthy of international protection.

Another huge factor contributing to Panama's distinction is the canal that splits it. Between 1904 and 1914, more than seventy-five thousand workers built a canal across the narrowest point of the Isthmus of

Panama, which is only 50 miles (81 km) wide. The Panama Canal changed history by allowing ships to sail from one ocean to the other without having to go around South America. Today the Panama Canal is known as "the gateway to the world."

TOPOGRAPHY

Despite its small size, Panama has a varied topography, including mountains, volcanoes, jungles, rain forests, islands, magnificent white beaches, plains, highlands, and lowlands.

MOUNTAINS When Panama emerged from the sea, volcanic intrusions created mountain peaks. These mountains form a continental divide—to the east of the divide, rivers flow to the Caribbean Sea; on the western side, rivers flow to the Pacific Ocean.

Panama has several mountain ranges. The Serranía de Tabasará begins near the Costa Rican border and ends in a region of low hills in the middle of the country, near the Panama Canal. This range contains Panama's highest point, the Volcán Barú, which is 11,400 feet (3,475 meters) high. Although this mountain is referred to as a volcano, it has been inactive for thousands of years. From its summit, one can see both the Atlantic and the Pacific Oceans.

The Cordillera de San Blas and the Serranía del Darién lie east of the canal. Toward the Colombian border, these two ranges become part of the Andes, the great chain of mountains in South America.

RAIN FORESTS Within several of the mountainous regions and along the Costa Rican and Colombian borders, Panama has dense rain forests. The Darién Gap is a vast region of rain forest and swamp in the eastern part of the country. The Chagres National Park boasts more than 1,000 species of plants, of which some 150 are native to that area.

The country's rain forests are lush, green regions filled with trees, winding rivers, and wildlife. Small villages are scattered throughout the forests. As few Panamanians reside in the humid and dense rain forests, some areas of the forests are virtually unexplored by humankind.

ISLANDS Panama has hundreds of small islands along the Atlantic and Pacific coasts. On the Atlantic side, the Panamanian coast meets the Caribbean Sea. Beyond the white sands of the Caribbean coast are 365 small islands called the San Blas Islands. Palm trees dot the small islands, and coral reefs surround them. Only 49 of the islands are inhabited, many of them home to the Guna people.

Along the Pacific coast of Panama are more than one thousand small islands, including Contadora, one of the Pearl Islands, and Taboga, which has about 1,500 inhabitants. The waters surrounding the Pacific islands are famous for fishing and other water sports.

PLAINS Parts of central Panama are flatter and are called lowlands or plains. The majority of rural Panamanians live in the lowlands, and the towns of Penomoné, Chitré, and Las Tablas are in this region. The large province of Chiriquí is also located in the lowlands of central Panama; however, parts of Chiriquí are mountainous. The lowlands have the longest dry season in Panama, but are still a productive area for agriculture.

A sandy beach on one of the San Blas islands is the picture of a tropical paradise.

The *flor del Espíritu Santo* is the national flower of Panama.

CLIMATE

Panama is generally hot and humid. Temperatures seldom fall below 79 degrees Fahrenheit (26 degrees Celsius) in the coolest months. It has two seasons—dry and rainy—and the weather conditions of these seasons vary from region to region. Temperatures on the Caribbean coast are slightly warmer than the Pacific coast. In the high mountainous regions, the climate is markedly cooler. In the Darién region, however, the temperature is often very high, even hotter than in the coastal regions.

RAINFALL

The rainy season runs from May to December and the dry season from January to April. The average rainfall in Panama varies from less than 51 inches (130 centimeters) to almost 120 inches (305 cm) per year. Moisture from the oceans and forests contributes substantially to the annual rainfall. Dense vegetation in the rain forests absorbs the water into its roots and sends water vapor into the atmosphere through transpiration, a process that resembles sweating. This water vapor increases the moisture in the air, raising humidity and forming clouds before falling to the ground as rain. As the trees are removed, water drains from the cleared areas, and the roots of the remaining trees cannot absorb as much water. As a result, the amount of water available for evaporation decreases, leading to less annual rainfall.

FLORA

Panama is host to some 1,400 native tree species and 9,900 species of other plants. The official national flower is the *flor del Espíritu Santo*, or "flower of the Holy Spirit." This flower is a beautiful white orchid that resembles a dove. Among the many plant species in Panama is the square tree. Found in the mountains to the west of Panama City, these trees have trunks that are an unusual square shape. Other plants found in Panama include small, fragrant frangipani (plumeria) trees and brightly flowered heliconia.

In the tropical rain forests, banana, mango, guava, cocoa, and plantain grow in abundance. A long, leafy grass called *chunga* proliferates there, and *guilpa* trees (giant, tangled trees with branches that form a canopy over the rivers) are a common sight. Snakelike vines grow on the guilpa trees, and other trees surrounding the guilpas also contribute to the dense forest.

Panama has a brilliantly colorful underwater world just off its shores. Plankton grows abundantly in the cold waters of the Pacific Ocean, while magnificent coral reefs thrive in the Caribbean's clear, warm waters.

FAUNA

Apart from its rich and varied flora, Panama is also home to thousands of wildlife species, many of which are unique to Panama. The country has nearly one thousand species of birds, including parrots and toucans that live in the wild.

A howler monkey in a tree is a common sight in the rain forest.

Less than a half-hour outside Panama City, bands of howler monkeys swing through the trees and inhabit the rain forests. These monkeys share the rain forests with over two hundred species of animals, including anteaters, pumas, jaguars, white-tailed deer, bats, iguanas, otters, opossums, crocodiles, and different types of rodents.

There are several unusual types of wildlife that can also be found in Panama, such as tapirs and golden frogs. The frogs are considered creatures of mystery and intrigue. They have skin that gleams, just like the color of gold. This rare species is found in the mountains west of Panama City. Measuring no more than 3 inches (7.62 cm) in length, the golden frogs are said to travel miles to congregate in a single pond during the mating season.

For centuries, Panama has been the nesting ground for thousands of migrating sea turtles. In the last decade, however, the number of turtles that

The skyline of Panama City is packed with high-rise buildings, many of them new.

have visited Panama has dropped. Many factors have caused this decline, including marine and beach pollution, the loss of nesting habitat to tourism activities, and the slaughter of turtles for commercial uses. People often kill the turtles for their eggs and meat, which are considered delicacies, while their shells are exported to Asian countries as jewelry.

RURAL AND URBAN PANAMA

Approximately 33 percent of the population lives in rural Panama. The majority of rural Panamanians are peasant farmers, ranchers, or teachers. Wealthy urban dwellers typically own large portions of rural land and hire peasant farmers to live on the terrain and cultivate it. By the late 1960s, many small farmers who owned their land sold it to the larger cattle ranches. Cattle ranches have expanded rapidly over the past few decades by absorbing rural land that was previously uninhabited.

PANAMA CITY The only Central American capital located on the Pacific Ocean is Panama City, the capital of Panama. The city was founded in 1519 and was once called Castillo del Oro, or "Castle of Gold." Today more than 1.5 million people live in metropolitan Panama City, a modern city of many high-rise buildings. The inhabitants of Panama City are commonly referred to as *capitalinos*.

Panama City is one of the few cities in the world with a protected tropical forest within its city limits. The Metropolitan Natural Park lies just fifteen minutes away from downtown Panama. This 655-acre (265-hectare) park can be seen from some of the city's high-rise apartments and serves as a peaceful retreat for urbanites.

PORTOBELO The beautiful town of Portobelo lies in a sheltered bay along Panama's Atlantic coast. Three forts surround the city: Fuerte Santiago, San Jerónimo, and San Fernando. The Panama Canal Company removed a fourth

The old Spanish Fort of Jerónimo in Portobelo is now a UNESCO World Heritage Site.

When the United States was building the Panama Canal, the popular slogan was "The Land Divided, A World United." Since the first ship passed through in 1914, the canal has linked the Atlantic and Pacific Oceans for all types of vessels. Hundreds of cruise ships pass through the canal each year, enabling tourists to enjoy the magnificent passage through pristine mountains, lakes, and locks. A typical journey through the 50-mile-long (80.5 km) canal lasts eight hours, but can take as long as fifteen hours if the ship has to wait for other vessels to pass through the canal. Ships may pass either way since the canal has three sets of parallel locks to handle traffic approaching from either ocean.

Ships have grown much larger than they were in 1914, however, and in recent years, many could no longer use the canal. In 2006, Panama began a huge expansion project to widen the canal. The construction was completed in 2016. The canal can now accommodate ships up to 1,200 feet (366 m) long and 160 feet (49 m) wide, which includes 99 percent of the world's container ships.

A ship sailing from the Atlantic Ocean to the Pacific Ocean enters the canal through Limón Bay. Before a ship enters the canal, a pilot from the Panama Canal Commission will board the ship to guide it through this channel of water. The captain then navigates the ship into the canal and along a 7-mile (11 km) passage to the Gatún Locks.

The Gatún Locks are three pairs of concrete chambers, resembling a staircase, that lift the ship to 85 feet (26 m) above sea level. Each lock chamber measures 1,000 feet (305 m) long and 110 feet (34 m) wide, about the size of the ship itself. Six electric locomotives, called mules, run along tracks on both sides of the locks. Attached to the ship, they guide it through the narrow locks. Canal workers release water from Gatún Lake on the other side of the Gatún Locks when the ship enters the first lock. This lifts the vessel to the same level as the next chamber. The process, which takes about ten minutes, continues through each of the locks until the ship is at Gatún Lake's level. Once the ship reaches Gatún Lake, canal workers detach the mules.

Gatún Lake is a quiet lake with small green islands that are home to animals, birds, and flowers. Ships have to pass through this beautiful 1.5-mile (2.5 km) waterway to reach the Gaillard Cut.

The Gaillard Cut is an 8-mile (12.9 km), human-made channel. It is bordered by green mountains that erupt with wild orchids at certain times of the year. The Pedro Miguel Locks are located at the end of the Gaillard Cut. In one step, the locks can lower the ship 31 feet (10 m) into Miraflores Lake.

The Miraflores Locks are two chambers that lower the ship to the same level as the Pacific Ocean. The engineers designed two locks at the Pacific end of the canal, because they believed that the underlying soil would not support one large lock. When the ship enters the first lock, canal workers release water to the  level of the second lock. The second chamber lowers the ship to sea level, and the height changes twice a day by about 12.5 feet (3.8 m).

After passing through the Miraflores Locks, the ship travels along another 8-mile (12.9 km) channel toward the end of the canal. The towns of Balboa, Balboa Heights, and La Boca are situated along this channel. Hundreds of pleasure boats also line this passageway. As the ship passes under the Bridge of the Americas, the canal pilot returns the wheel to the ship's captain. The vessel then enters the Pacific Ocean.

The beautiful city of Portobelo is a port on the Caribbean coast.

fort in 1910 so that the stone could be used in the locks of the canal. Today Portobelo has a population of only 4,560 or so, and houses the religious statue of the Black Christ. However, its historical significance makes it one of Panama's most intriguing cities.

The first European to discover Portobelo was Christopher Columbus, when he took refuge in the bay in 1502. Within one hundred years, Portobelo became a great trading center between Spain and its colonies in the New World. The plentiful gold and treasures in the Americas were shipped to the ports and loaded into galleons bound for Spain. Portobelo was attacked many times by English sailors and buccaneers, so Spain eventually decided to use a different port to ship its treasures. Consequently, Portobelo's importance declined.

In present-day Portobelo, windowless tin-roofed houses with black walls are a common sight. However, the town of Portobelo still retains its historical charm as it reminds visitors of a long-forgotten time.

The ruins of Spanish colonial forts in the city, along with nearby Fort San Lorenzo, were designated as a UNESCO World Heritage Site in 1980. The site is named the "Fortifications on the Caribbean Side of Panama: Portobelo-San Lorenzo." The World Heritage organization describes the fortifications as "Magnificent examples of seventeenth- and eighteenth-century military architecture, these Panamanian forts on the Caribbean coast form part of the defense system built by the Spanish Crown to protect transatlantic trade." In 2012, the site was also added to the List of World Heritage in Danger, because of the threat of uncontrolled urban development in the region, environmental dangers, and a general lack of maintenance.

COLÓN At the Atlantic end of the Panama Canal lies Colón, Panama's second-largest city. Like Panama City, Colón is located within the Panama Canal Zone, an area that was under US control until 1997.

Panamanians named Colón in honor of Christopher Columbus, while the US citizens who were in Panama to build a railroad in the mid-1800s called the city Aspinwall. For many years, people referred to the city by both names. Eventually the name Colón became the official name after Panamanians refused to acknowledge and deliver mail to the city of "Aspinwall."

INTERNET LINKS

www.bbc.com/news/magazine-28756378
"Silent Darien: The gap in the world's longest road" is an article, with maps and photos, about the Panamanian gap in the Pan-American Highway.

news.nationalgeographic.com/news/2014/08/140815-panama-canal-culebra-cut-lake-gatun-focus
The article, "A Hundred Years Old Today, the Panama Canal Is About to Get a Lot Bigger," includes maps, photos, and graphics about the recent expansion of the canal.

whc.unesco.org/en/list/135
This is the UNESCO page for the Fortifications on the Caribbean Side of Panama: Portobelo-San Lorenzo.

whc.unesco.org/en/list/159
This is the description of the Darién National Park World Heritage Site, along with a photo gallery.

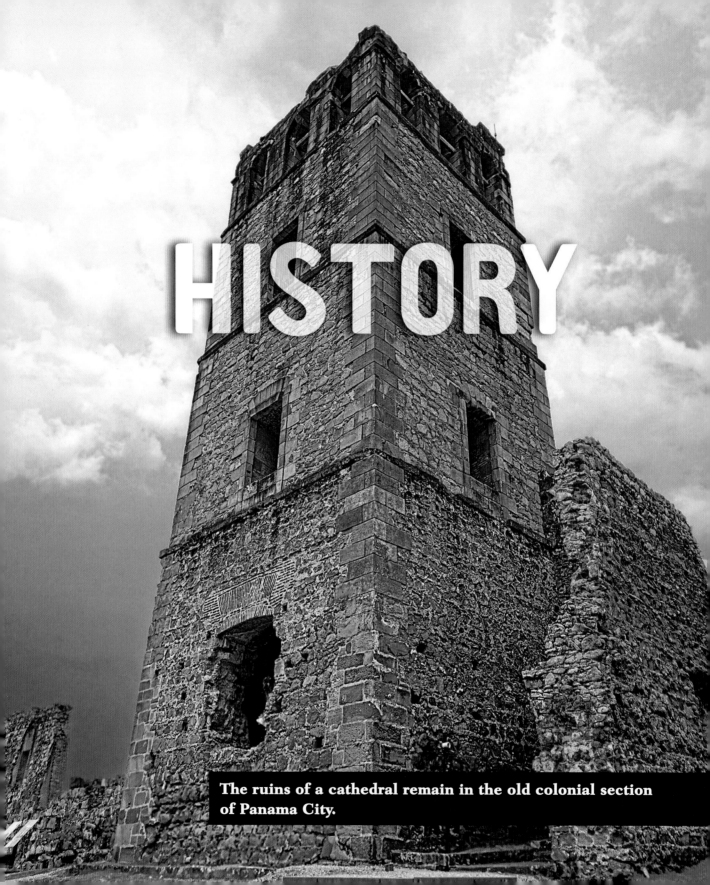

HISTORY

The ruins of a cathedral remain in the old colonial section of Panama City.

2

BEFORE THE SPANISH ARRIVED ON the Isthmus of Panama, the land was home to a thriving population of Native people. No one knows how many indigenous people lived in the region because there is no documentation, and historians' estimates range from two hundred thousand to two million. Nevertheless, archaeological discoveries, as well as the written descriptions by early European explorers, point to a number of flourishing native communities and cultures on the isthmus.

Three main groups of people lived there. The Ngöbe-Buglés, who were related to the Maya of Mexico, lived near the modern Costa Rican border. The Emberás lived in western Panama, and the Guna (also spelled Kuna or Cuna) people resided along the Caribbean coastal region of Guna Yala, and the San Blas Islands. These groups lived in circular, thatched houses, and cultivated vegetables and fruit.

In 1501 Rodrigo de Bastidas became the first European to set foot in Panama. A year later, Christopher Columbus established a trading post at Portobelo. Early Spanish explorers in search of gold and treasure almost wiped out the Panamanian Natives through a combination of transmitted diseases, slavery, and indiscriminate killing.

BALBOA SEES THE PACIFIC

In this old print, Spanish conquistador Vasco Núñez de Balboa claims the Pacific Ocean for Spain.

In 1510 Vasco Núñez de Balboa, a Spanish explorer and a member of Bastidas's crew, settled in the Darién region. Along with other Spanish settlers, he founded the first successful Spanish settlement on the mainland of the Americas, Santa María la Antigua del Darién. (The settlement's location is in present-day Colombia.) The Spanish king appointed Balboa as the governor of the region, and Balboa embarked upon a series of exploratory expeditions of the region. He was searching for both gold and slaves in the Native territories when he heard of the existence of a great sea to the south. On September 25, 1513, he and his party of 190 Spanish soldiers became the first Europeans to cross the Isthmus of Panama and see the Pacific Ocean, which Balboa claimed for Spain.

The discovery that the isthmus is a narrow land bridge between the Atlantic and the Pacific led the Spanish to build a trade route from one side to the other. Goods from and bound for Spain were sent by ship to the isthmus, hauled across the land, and loaded onto a new ship on the other side. The route became known as *El Camino Real*, or the "Royal Road."

When Balboa returned to the Antigua settlement in 1514, he found that the Spanish King Ferdinand had appointed a new governor named Pedro Arias de Dávila, or Pedrarias. Wanting his popular rival out of the way, in 1518, Pedrarias falsely charged Balboa with treason, arrested him, and had him beheaded. Pedrarias killed or enslaved thousands of indigenous people, for which he gained the notorious nickname "Pedrarias the Cruel." His brutal treatment of the Natives enraged a priest named Bartolomé de las Casas, who suggested that King Charles V of Spain export over four thousand African slaves to Panama to replace the local ones. (De las Casas reportedly came to regret that suggestion.) This marked the beginning of the slave trade to Central America, a practice that lasted more than two hundred years.

In 1519, Pedrarias abandoned Santa María la Antigua del Darién and moved his capital to a fishing village on the Pacific Coast that the Natives called *Panama*, meaning "plenty of fish." This settlement would grow to become Panama City. It quickly became an important trade center and transit point for the exportation of silver and gold back to Spain, as well as a hub for Spanish expeditions into South America.

THE SPANISH COLONY

From the sixteenth century until 1821, Spain retained control of Panama. In 1538 Spain established an *audiencia* (ow-dee-EHN-see-ah), or court, in Panama to administer Spanish territory that stretched from Nicaragua to Cape Horn. Because the area of this audiencia was so vast, Spain established a new audiencia in 1563 to control the area that now constitutes the country of Panama.

TRADE MONOPOLY With Panama as one of its many New World colonies, Spain retained a virtual monopoly on the trade of riches from colonies around the Pacific Ocean. The other European countries challenged this monopoly and began to attack the Panamanian ports. Sir Francis Drake, an English buccaneer, attacked the ports, ambushed mule trains on the Royal Road, and also looted the coastal cities from 1572 until 1596.

In 1597 Spain moved its Atlantic port to Portobelo. Sir Henry Morgan, another English buccaneer, held this port for ransom in 1668. He looted Panama City before burning it. To halt the thousands of deaths and the destruction of cities, Spain signed a treaty with England in 1670 to defend the New World together. However, the peace was short-lived as both countries were soon fighting again.

ENGLISH INTERVENTION Spain retained control over Panama, but, in 1713, England secured the right to supply slaves to the Spanish colonies. Using this right, England smuggled trade goods aboard the slave ships, which in turn weakened Spain's economic control over the isthmus. Spanish colonists who regarded Panama as their homeland, and who wanted independence from the Spanish reign, assisted the English in forming a contraband trade based in Jamaica. To combat its diminished control over the Panamanians, Spain made the Panamanian audiencia a part of the viceroyalty of New Granada, an audiencia that encompassed Colombia, Venezuela, and Ecuador.

In 1739 Spain and England went to war, and the English destroyed Portobelo. Without the trade route through Portobelo, Spain lost much of its interest in Panama. The economy declined with the loss of Panama's status as a trade center. This downturn was crippling to the colony primarily because the Panamanians had neglected to develop another economic base.

INDEPENDENCE After the Spanish-English war of 1739, many Spanish colonies enlisted England's help to separate from Spain.

Simón Bolívar eventually defeated Spain and liberated New Granada in 1819. The Spanish governor fled Colombia and ruled in Panama until 1821. When the Spanish ruler died, another took his place for a short period of time and then left a Panamanian as the acting governor. On November 28, 1821, Panama declared its independence from Spain and became a part of the short-lived country of Gran Colombia.

From 1819 to 1831, Gran Colombia included the territories of present-day Panama, Colombia, Venezuela, Ecuador, northern Peru, and parts of Guyana and Brazil. Politically, the larger nation could not hold itself together, and it soon dissolved into Venezuela, Ecuador, and New Granada, which was made up of present-day Panama and Colombia. The Republic of New Granada would go through several more names before becoming the present-day Republic of Colombia in 1886. Panama remained a part of Colombia until it seceded in 1903.

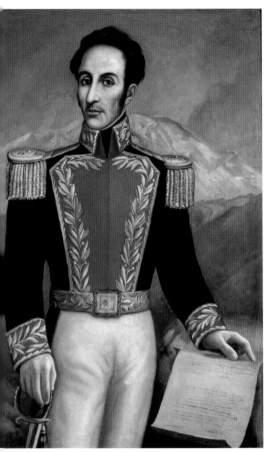

Simón Bolívar hoped to unite the newly independent Spanish American republics in the early nineteenth century.

COLOMBIAN CONTROL, 1821-1903

Although Panama declared independence from Spain in 1821, Colombia controlled it from 1821 to 1903. Simón Bolívar, who was also the president of Peru (1824—1826), assumed dictatorial responsibilities, and continued his attempt to unite the Spanish American republics, while others proposed a single vast monarchy.

In his pursuit of complete independence from Spanish attacks, Bolívar requested protection from Britain. He invited Britain, as well as several other countries including the United States, to attend a conference in Panama in 1826. At this conference, he proposed a treaty that would enjoin Gran Colombia, Mexico, Central America, and Peru to defend one another and peacefully settle disputes. Colombia ratified the treaty, but it never became effective, and Bolívar died of tuberculosis in 1830 without seeing a united government. From 1830 to 1903, Panamanian attempts to break from Colombian control were unsuccessful.

INDEPENDENCE FROM COLOMBIA

With United States backing, Panama proclaimed its independence from Colombia in 1903. A Panamanian named José Augustín Arango organized a revolutionary junta to overthrow the Colombian government. Arango knew that the United States wanted to construct a canal across Panama. He persuaded the United States to support Panamanian independence to ensure that commercial gains would be retained by Panama.

Under the Hay-Bunau-Varilla Treaty, the United States gained ownership of the canal, 10 miles (16 km) of controlled zone around it, and the right to intervene in Panamanian politics in exchange for holding back Colombian troops. Panama objected, but gave in after the United States threatened to withdraw its support. On November 6, 1903, President Theodore Roosevelt recognized Arango's junta as the de facto government, and Panama became an independent protectorate of the United States. Panama had finally achieved independence, but at a high price.

CROSSING THE ISTHMUS

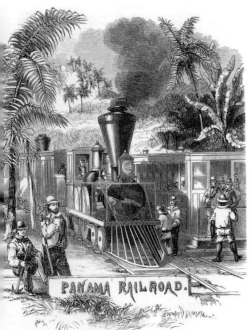

A wood engraving from 1870 illustrates a train on the Panama Railroad.

Almost from the moment Vasco de Balboa gazed upon the Pacific Ocean in 1513, people began to dream of building a waterway across the isthmus. As early as 1534, King Charles V of Spain ordered a survey for a route through the Americas that would ease the voyage for ships traveling between Spain and Peru. The ocean voyage around South America was not only time consuming but extremely perilous, particularly in the waters off Cape Horn. This region at the southernmost tip of mainland South America was well known as a "sailors' graveyard" due to its powerful winds, strong currents, large waves, and icebergs.

For centuries, the Royal Road served as a major trade route over the isthmus. The trail was hardly a modern highway, however, and the overland route was difficult and dangerous.

THE GOLD RUSH AND THE RAILROAD In 1848, gold was discovered in California. Rather than travel across the United States, some prospectors sailed from the eastern United States to Panama, crossed overland to the Pacific, and sailed on another ship to California.

On January 28, 1855, a railroad across the isthmus was completed. Some twelve thousand workers died during the five years it took to build the railroad, particularly from malaria and yellow fever. Only 47 miles (76 km) long, the railroad required 304 bridges and culverts over difficult terrain. The railroad earned more than $7 million dollars in its first six years, but the completion of a US transcontinental railroad in 1869 ended the golden years for the Panamanian railroad.

THE FRENCH CANAL During the nineteenth century, several countries, including the United States, Britain, and France, discussed building a canal across Panama or Nicaragua. The French engineer Ferdinand de Lesseps formed a canal company in 1879 to build a canal in Panama. He planned to complete it within twelve to eighteen years.

He officially began the project on January 1, 1880, but did not begin the work until 1881. By 1885, just 10 percent of the project was completed and only about 20 percent of the workers were healthy enough to continue. As with the building of the railroad, malaria and yellow fever claimed a huge number of lives, in this case more than twenty-two thousand. De Lesseps's company went bankrupt in 1888 due to the workers' bad health and his refusal to build a canal in which the levels would vary across the terrain. In 1889 work stopped on the canal, and thousands of workers, mostly black men from the West Indies, were unemployed.

THE PANAMA CANAL

For centuries, different countries had wanted to build a canal across Panama to link the world's largest oceans—the Atlantic and Pacific. In 1529, a Spanish priest drew the first plans for a canal, but Spain refused to build a canal that would help other nations. A famous explorer, Alexander von Humboldt, designed another plan for the canal in 1811, but lacked the technology to materialize his dream. From 1870 to 1875 the United States drafted seven possible routes for a Panamanian canal.

A few years after de Lesseps's project failed, the US Senate ratified a treaty with Panama on February 23, 1904, which enabled the United States to build the canal. President Theodore Roosevelt appointed a commission to oversee the project. The commission hired John Findley Wallace, a fifty-one-year-old civil engineer, to design the canal, and William C. Gorgas, an army doctor, to supervise all hospital and sanitary work.

BUILDING THE CANAL Unhappy with the intolerable working conditions and the commission's inability to progress on the canal, Wallace quit and Roosevelt appointed John Stevens as the new engineer in 1905. Stevens began excavating in 1906 and soon discovered that he needed to build a lock canal, rather than a canal at sea level. However, he resigned in 1907.

During the first few years of construction, Gorgas fought to eliminate yellow fever, malaria, and other deadly diseases that were killing the workers. He started a sanitation project that supplied running water to all the towns

In this 1913 photograph of the construction of the Panama Canal, workers drill holes for dynamite as they cut through bedrock in the mountains of Panama.

in the Canal Zone, established hospitals, destroyed the breeding grounds of disease-carrying mosquitoes, and fumigated homes. By 1906 Gorgas had successfully eliminated yellow fever and malaria. In the process, he probably saved at least seventy-one thousand lives. Nevertheless, thousands of workers died building the canal.

After Stevens's resignation, Lieutenant Colonel George Goethels took over as chief engineer. He supervised the digging of the Culebra Cut, a channel through the mountains, at a cost of $14 million. First a dam was built to trap the water from the Chagres River into the lake created at Gatún. Then they built three double sets of locks, the Gatún Locks, Pedro Miguel Locks, and Miraflores Locks, to raise the ships from sea level to the level of Gatún Lake—almost 85 feet (26 m) above sea level—and back down to sea level again.

The Ancón was the first ship to pass through the completed Panama Canal on August 15, 1914. After this maiden voyage, the Culebra Cut was renamed

The history of the Panama Canal is summed up in eight short words in a famously clever palindrome—"A man, a plan, a canal—Panama!" A palindrome is a word, phrase, or sentence that reads the same backward as forward, as in the words mom, kayak, *and* noon. *In a palindromic phrase or sentence, the letters must remain in the same order, but can be grouped differently, and punctuation can be changed, as in "Madam, I'm Adam." Palindromes don't necessarily have to make sense, but the best ones do.*

"A man, a plan, a canal—Panama!" is one of the most famous palindromes ever because it not only makes sense but literally tells a true story, with US president Teddy Roosevelt usually considered the "man with a plan." Note that this palindrome works only in English!

No one knows for certain who first came up with this play on words, but it was first published in 1948 by the British mathematician Leigh Mercer in Notes and Queries.

the Gaillard Cut, in honor of David du Bose Gaillard who oversaw the blasting of the mountains. In 1966, channel lighting was added to allow ships to pass through twenty-four hours a day. The Bridge of the Americas, a mile-long highway, was built over the canal to connect Panama City with the west side of the canal. In 2016, Panama completed a major upgrade to the canal which allows today's larger vessels to use it.

Today the Panama Canal is a living monument to the seventy-five thousand people who worked on it, and to those who died while building a passageway between the Atlantic and Pacific Oceans.

QUALIFIED INDEPENDENCE

Under the 1903 Hay-Bunau-Varilla Treaty, the newly independent country of Panama gave the United States the right to use, occupy, and control, in perpetuity, the land upon which it built the Panama Canal, as well as sovereign rights within the Canal Zone.

Panama adopted a constitution in 1904 that was similar to the US constitution. In 1925, the Guna rebelled. Subsequently, the United

In 1964, students demonstrate in Panama City against the US presence in the Canal Zone.

States intervened and convinced the Panamanian government and the Gunas to sign a treaty that recognized the San Blas Islands as a semiautonomous territory.

Panamanians, for the most part, resented US involvement in their government and daily lives. After intervening several times in the 1910s and 1920s, President Franklin D. Roosevelt proposed a principle of nonintervention in Panama, and Congress accepted it in 1936. The two countries signed a treaty that same year to end the protectorate and the United States' right to intervene. The treaty, however, did not alter US sovereignty in the Canal Zone.

THE NEW REPUBLIC OF PANAMA

During World War II, the United States occupied 134 sites in the republic, including an airfield, a naval base, and several radar stations. In 1946, after the war, the United States wanted to keep the bases for another twenty years, and Panama acceded to the request. This decision incited ten thousand Panamanians to revolt, ultimately resulting in the deaths of several students and police.

Due to the intense clash, the United States evacuated all its bases in Panama and outside the Canal Zone, and did not reoccupy them until 1955. This clash was to be the first of several confrontations between angry students protesting the US presence in their country and the Panamanian police. In 1958, a violent riot killed nine people. Another riot in 1959 prompted the United States to build a fence around the Canal Zone. In 1960 the United States agreed to fly the Panamanian flag in the Canal Zone, but several US residents living within the Zone refused to fly the flag. On January 9, 1964, almost two hundred Panamanian students stormed into the Zone with

On May 12, 1968, Panamanians reelected Arnulfo Arias as their president. Arias, who had served controversially in this role several times since 1940, resumed his presidential role on October 1, 1968. On October 11, the National Guard (part of the Panamanian military) removed Arias from his position following his attempt to dismiss two senior officers. The country fell into disarray for several months until General Omar Torrijos took control.

Although he had taken power by means of a military coup, Torrijos proved to be an effective and popular leader. The son of schoolteachers, he referred to himself as a "populist," a government leader who represents and supports the common people. He reached out to rural Panamanians, a group that hadn't previously been involved in the government.

As the head of the government, Torrijos instituted widespread changes in education, health care, public transportation, social programs, and foreign investment. Most Panamanians adored Torrijos, but his opponents called him a tyrant because his improvements came at the cost of military rule. In 1978, Torrijos stepped down as head of the government but remained as head of the National Guard. The national assembly appointed Aristides Royo as president.

On July 31, 1981, Torrijos's life came to an abrupt end when his plane crashed in the mountains of western Panama. He was fifty-two years old. The cause of the crash has never been determined, but many people believe that General Manuel Noriega, who worked closely with Torrijos and later replaced him, planted a bomb aboard the small airplane. Others, including Noriega himself, claim the United States was behind the crash, which was remarkably similar to one which had killed Ecuador's president Jaime Roldós a mere two months before. Documents detailing investigations into the Torrijos crash disappeared during the US invasion of Panama on December 20, 1989, and haven't surfaced since. Questions about the death of Torrijos remain to this day. Theories abound regarding the role of the US Central Intelligence Agency (CIA), but nothing has ever been proven.

Meanwhile, Torrijos's supporters have paid tribute to him on every anniversary of his death, and have also turned his former residence into a history museum. He was one of the most important figures in Panamanian history, and his legacy continues today.

their flag. After a struggle during which their flag was torn, thousands of Panamanians charged across the border fence and rioted. The three-day riot killed more than twenty people, injured hundreds, and strained diplomatic relations between the two countries.

After the riots and continuing public dissatisfaction, Panama requested new treaties, but the United States stalled negotiations by citing internal reasons for the delay. Under the leadership of US President Jimmy Carter and General Omar Torrijos of Panama, the two countries finally signed a treaty on September 7, 1977, that gave Panama full control of the canal on December 31, 1999. They also signed another treaty, which guaranteed that the canal would remain neutral and open "to peaceful transit by all vessels of all nations on terms of entire equality." However, the new treaty also gave the United States and Panama priority to the canal during wartime.

THE RISE AND FALL OF MANUEL NORIEGA

After Torrijos died in 1981, General Manuel Antonio Noriega (b. 1934) became head of the National Guard and took control of the government. Noriega had been a secret CIA informant since the 1950s. From that time through the 1990s, the CIA was covertly working in Central and South America to counter the spread of leftist movements and governments friendly to Cuba's Fidel Castro and the Soviet Union.

An example of how Noriega aided the CIA is illustrated by the infamous Iran-Contra Affair that took place during the administration of US president Ronald Reagan. In the 1980s, the CIA was deeply involved in fighting revolutionaries in Nicaragua. Iran-Contra was a clandestine arrangement in which funds from covert US weapons sales to Iran (which was under an arms embargo at the time) were diverted to Contra (counter-revolutionary) guerrilla groups fighting in Nicaragua. Noriega helped to facilitate this transfer of funds.

Noriega was also a major cocaine trafficker, a fact which was well-known to the United States but overlooked because of his usefulness to the CIA. Astute and ruthless, Noriega expanded the military, which he renamed as the Panama Defense Forces, and greatly increased its power.

The Noriega years witnessed widespread corruption, repression and murder of political opposition, and a troubled economy. He rigged the elections and used the military for personal gain. Noriega is said to have established a "narcokleptocracy" in Panama, with a kleptocracy ("rule by thieves") being defined as a government ruled by officials who pocket the state's funds as their own personal wealth. A narcokleptocracy, by extension, is a government run by drug traffickers.

Noriega's relationship with the United States soured as he extended his brutal power—particularly after the botched 1989 Panamanian presidential election in which Noriega's attempt to rig the outcome became public. When the opposition candidate Guillermo Endara became the clear winner, Noriega voided the election. He remained in control until the United States invaded Panama on December 20, 1989, and forced Noriega to surrender and face drug trafficking charges in the United States.

General Manuel Noriega decries US aggression in 1988 in Panama City.

ROCKIN' WARFARE

One of the stranger episodes in the unsavory relationship between the United States and Manuel Noriega took place during the US invasion of Panama in December 1989.

To avoid capture by the US troops, Noriega took refuge in the Vatican Embassy in Panama City on the fifth day of the invasion, which happened to be Christmas Day. (The Vatican is a sovereign city-state located in Rome, Italy, and is the seat of the Roman Catholic Church.) Noriega was hoping the Church would provide him with sanctuary in Vatican City itself. Since international law prohibited the troops from entering the embassy, the US Army resorted to "psychological warfare" to flush him out—it played some rock music.

The army surrounded the embassy and blasted nonstop rock music at "deafening levels" twenty-four hours a day for three days. Among the heavy metal songs played repeatedly were "Panama" by Van Halen, "We're Not Gonna Take It" by Twisted Sister, and "Welcome to the Jungle" by Guns N'Roses.

Whether the loud music rattled Noriega himself is not clear. Reportedly, he was cooped up inside the embassy in a "stark" room without air conditioning or TV, alone with only a Bible for reading matter. But the embassy staff was not amused. The pope's representatives complained to US president George H.W. Bush, and the musical assault stopped.

Meanwhile, the United States and Vatican officials negotiated fiercely to find a way to get Noriega out of the embassy. The Vatican had no intention of granting political asylum to Noriega, but could not force him to leave the embassy. The Vatican ambassador, Monsignor Jose Sebastian Laboa, convinced the dictator to give himself up. Noriega surrendered on January 3, 1990.

NORIEGA'S FATE

Noriega was tried in Miami, Florida, and found guilty on eight counts of drug trafficking and money laundering. He served seventeen years of his thirty-year prison sentence in Florida, and was released in 2007. However, the government of France had also convicted him of money laundering in a 1999 trial *in absentia*, and requested his extradition to serve prison time there.

In 2010, after some legal wrangling, Noriega began a ten-year prison sentence in France. However, Panama wanted its former dictator back, and requested that France extradite him to face justice for human rights violations committed during his reign. France concurred and in 2011, the aging, frail prisoner was incarcerated at El Renacer prison on the outskirts of Panama City. Although the prison has a reputation for its dreadful living conditions, Noriega lives in a one-bedroom apartment with air conditioning, a television, and a computer.

In 2015, Noriega appeared on Panamanian television, apologized, and requested a pardon or permission to serve out his remaining time under house arrest, perhaps at the home of one of his daughters.

INTERNET LINKS

www.bbc.com/news/world-latin-america-15853540
This BBC article provides a good look at Manuel Noriega's career.

www.lonelyplanet.com/panama/history#215505
This site offers a good overview of Panama's history, along with a timeline.

www.nytimes.com/1981/08/02/obituaries/panama-leader-killed-in-crash-in-bad-weather.html
The obituary of General Omar Torrijos in 1981 tells the story of one of Panama's most important leaders.

GOVERNMENT

The Presidential Palace is decked with the national colors of blue, white, and red.

3

PANAMA'S POLITICAL CLIMATE HAS changed enormously in the past quarter century. Coming out of the years of military dictatorship, and particularly the twenty-one-year reign of strongman Manuel Noriega, the Republic of Panama is now a constitutional democracy in fact as well as name. Panamanians observe two independence days—on November 3, they celebrate independence from Colombia, and on November 28, independence from Spain.

On December 31, 1999, Panama celebrated another form of independence—winning political jurisdiction over their entire country, which came about with the return of the Panama Canal by the United States. That date marked the end of nearly one hundred years of US control of the canal.

Panama maintains a limited national security force with air and maritime capabilities. However, it has no standing army. In 1990, following the demise of Manuel Noriega's reign, the government abolished Panama's military. Panama became the second Latin American country, after Costa Rica, to permanently do away with its standing army.

Panama's constitution, which was amended in 1983, 1994, and 2004, provides for three branches of government: executive, legislative, and judicial. The people elect a president and a vice president every five years, while the president appoints the cabinet of ministers. Nine judges are appointed by the president to serve ten-year terms on the Supreme Court. The legislature is the National Assembly (*Asamblea Nacional*). It is made up of seventy-one representatives, each elected for a five-year term. Voting age in Panama is eighteen and everyone is required to vote. However, there are no penalties for those who don't.

Although the people elect the legislative and executive officials every five years, the 1968 coup d'état by the National Guard established an indirect military control of the government that lasted until 1990. The 1968 coup brought General Omar Torrijos to power. Under General Manuel Antonio Noriega Morena, the National Guard became the Panama Defense Forces, or *Fuerzas de Defensa de Panama* (FDP), in the 1980s. The National Guard and FDP essentially controlled the government for more than twenty years by handpicking presidential and legislative candidates, then ensuring their victory through fraud or by removing the FDP opponent from office after the election. After Noriega's downfall, however, the FDP lost its de facto control of the government, and the constitution's democratic principles once again became the law.

The Ministry of Government and Justice building in Panama City

RECENT PRESIDENTIAL ELECTIONS

On the day of the invasion, a new president, Guillermo Endara, from the leading Arnulfista Party (now the Panameñista Party), was sworn in. The 1994 election brought a surprise victory to Ernesto Pérez Balladares, who was a member of Noriega's former party. He instituted a program of economic reform to create more employment and attract foreign investment. In 1999,

Mireya Elisa Moscoso de Gruber, the widow of former president Arnulfo Arias, became the next president.

Martín Torrijos, who served as president from 2004 to 2009, is the son of Omar Torrijos. He won the presidency in 2004 after pledging to fight corruption, lower the unemployment rate, modernize the Panama Canal, and investigate alleged human rights violations that were committed during his father's rule. He introduced a plan to expand the Panama Canal to accommodate larger cargo ships, a project that was approved by referendum on October 22, 2006. Despite his popularity, Torrijos was not able to run for reelection because Panama's constitution forbids consecutive second terms.

Conservative businessman Ricardo Martinelli followed as the next president in 2009, winning the election with 61 percent of the vote. He turned out to be an immensely popular president who significantly improved Panama's economic situation, raising productivity and reducing poverty by increasing the minimum wage to the highest level in Latin America. Martinelli also arranged to bring Manuel Noriega back to Panama to serve prison time there.

In 2014, Juan Carlos Varela of the Panameñista Party, became Panama's newest president. He won by 39 percent of the vote against José Domingo Arias, despite Arias's support by Ricardo Martinelli's Democratic Change (*Cambio Democrático*) Party. The next election will take place in 2019.

PANAMA'S CONSTITUTION

Adopted in 1904, Panama's first constitution was similar to the US Constitution. The constitution that Panama adopted in 1976 remains in force today, most recently amended in 2004.

President Juan Carlos Varela delivers a speech on June 24, 2016, at the opening of the new Cocoli Locks of the Panama Canal expansion.

The constitution guarantees the personal rights of Panama's citizens. These personal rights include the freedom of speech and press, the right to form political parties and other professional or civic groups without government interference, freedom of religion, freedom to move within the country, and to leave and return to the country, as well as the right for a citizen who is charged with a crime to have legal representation. Panama's constitution also establishes the procedures for electing and appointing government officials.

Panamanians vote in the 2009 presidential election.

Local government is organized according to the country's ten provinces, and three *comarcas*, or autonomous indigenous regions. Each province is headed by a governor and is divided into districts and townships, including ten cities. Voters in these jurisdictions choose mayors and councilors to administer their respective areas.

PANAMANIAN LAWS

Panama has many laws, including civil, criminal, and labor codes. After years of tyranny by the National Guard and FDP, the government has stressed human rights in the home, workplace, and prison. Former president Martín Torrijos (in office 2004—2009) passed several laws that make the government more transparent. He formed the National Anti-Corruption Council, whose members represent the highest levels of government, as well as civil society, labor organizations, and religious leadership.

THE GUNAS' SELF-GOVERNMENT

In 1925 the Guna people rebelled against the government and declared themselves an independent state. Today the Gunas live in the politically autonomous region of Guna Yala (formerly known as San Blas) in Panama. The province includes fifty-one communities, many of which are located on islands of the San Blas Archipelago off the northern coast of Panama. Each community is led by a spiritual and political leader called the sahila, *or chief. The region as a whole is governed by the Guna General Congress, which is led by three* Sahila Dummagan *("Great Sahilas").*

The Gunas' political life revolves around a nightly gathering of the community. During a gathering, the Guna men, who form the congress, meet with the sahila to discuss business, delegate duties, and recall religious and historical traditions. These gatherings also enable the Gunas to discuss and resolve any disputes among group members through mutual consensus. According to Guna law, an individual who commits a wrong against another member of the group must speak before the group at the gathering. Otherwise the group will not rescrutinize, replay, recollect, or recall the wrong.

Several times each year, every village sends at least one chief and another member of the village group to a general congress. The general congress holds a gathering similar to the ones in the individual villages where they exchange information and resolve matters or disputes.

INTERNET LINKS

www.panama-offshore-services.com/blog/guide_to_panama_political_parties.htm
This site describes Panama's current political parties and their positions.

www.presidencia.gob.pa/en
This is the official government site of the Republic of Panama, in English.

www.tripadvisor.com/Travel-g298434-c2329/San-Blas-Islands:Panama:Kuna.Cultures.html
This overview of Guna culture includes a look at their political structure.

ECONOMY

A balboa, the $1 coin, is surrounded by other Panamanian coins.

4

OVER THE PAST DECADE, PANAMA has had one of the fastest-growing economies in the world. The country has a free market economy based mainly on the services sector—especially banking, commerce, and tourism. The US hand over of the Panama Canal in 1999 has been a particularly positive factor for the economy, and Panama's recent expansion of the canal has contributed to economic growth and should continue to do so. In addition, Panama City's new rapid transit system, which began service with one line in 2014, is being expanded with an additional seven lines to be completed by 2040. This project is part of a national plan to improve transportation systems in Panama that should further boost its economy.

The balboa, named after the great explorer and Panamanian leader Vasco Núñez de Balboa, is the Panamanian currency. It circulates only in coin. The US dollar is the paper currency. One balboa is equivalent to one US dollar, and one hundred centesimos constitute one balboa.

A container ship travels through the Miraflores Locks in 2015.

UPS AND DOWNS

Historically, Panama's key location between two continents and two oceans has benefited its economy. Beginning in the early 1500s, settlers and sailors used the isthmus to transport goods from the Pacific Ocean to the Atlantic Ocean. The port cities prospered during Spain's colonial trade and became dependent on world commerce for their prosperity. The flow of goods also discouraged Panamanians from producing their own products.

Until the late twentieth century, Panama's economy fluctuated according to international trade cycles. Pirate raids in the 1700s caused Spain to stop using Panama's ports to transport goods, and led to a sharp decline in the Panamanian economy. When gold was discovered in California in the 1800s, Panama's economy boomed as thousands of gold prospectors sailed into its Atlantic ports and traveled across the country on foot or by railway.

When the United States built a transcontinental railroad, Panama's economy again declined. However, in the late 1800s and early 1900s, the country's economy surged as first France and then the United States started construction of the canal. During the worldwide depression in the 1930s, the economy sank once again.

World War II stimulated Panama's economy because US forces moved onto the isthmus. The economy continued to expand after the war, due to the rise in canal-linked activities, agricultural output, banana exports, and a sophisticated commercial and retail system. Today the economy is still largely dependent on canal-related businesses.

PANAMA'S FINANCIAL SYSTEM

CURRENCY The US involvement in Panama's past is evident in its money—the official currency in Panama is the US dollar. As the official currency, the dollar is the principal means of exchange, and an important source for attracting foreign capital. The dollar has contributed to Panama's low inflation rate, averaging 3.99 percent between 2008 and 2016, which is one of the lowest in Latin America. The freedom to move funds in and out of the country without charge has also contributed to Panama's stable environment.

TAX SYSTEM During President Ricardo Martinelli's term, he raised the sales tax from 5 percent to 7 percent to increase revenues to pay for infrastructure projects. Panama has a territorial tax system—that is, it only taxes profits earned within the country. For instance, if a Panamanian company makes a profit through international trade, the profit is tax-exempt. This tax-exempt status on international profits encourages the growth of international and commercial banking activities within Panama. Furthermore, the government will not tax the interest on deposits and bonds that are registered at the local exchange rates. This policy encourages corporations and individuals to deposit profits in Panamanian banks.

BANKING Panama is one of the world's most important banking hubs. In 2015, the International Banking Center in Panama reported total assets in the order of $118,477 million, 9.2 percent more than in 2014. Panama became an international banking center during the Torrijos years. Foreign

Panama City is a center for the financial services industry.

banks are attracted to Panama's dollar-based economy, its historical status as a trade center, and its low taxation policy on deposits and income.

During the Noriega years, the banking sector developed into a money-laundering service for the drug trade, but when the country returned to democracy, the banks regained their international status.

Panama's secrecy laws, which prohibit banks from disclosing information about their customers, also help attract many clients. Foreign investors often deposit funds in Panamanian banks that they wish to keep secret from some agency, such as the Internal Revenue Service. In recent years, however, Panama has been trying to change its reputation as a tax haven, signing treaties with other nations aimed at eliminating tax evasion.

EMPLOYMENT

Panama's labor force numbers about 1.6 million people, but there remains a shortage of skilled labor and an oversupply of unskilled labor. Nevertheless, the unemployment rate is relatively low at 4.5 percent.

One of the nation's largest employers since the beginning of the twentieth century has been the Panama Canal. It contributes to more than 30 percent of the gross domestic product (GDP) and continues to generate more jobs, businesses, and government revenues than any other source in the country.

A large majority of Panamanians work in the services sector (77 percent). This sector includes the Panama Canal, logistics, banking, the Colón Free Trade Zone, insurance, container ports, flagship registry, and tourism in addition to the usual service divisions. Panama's services-based economy benefits greatly from the Colón Free Zone, which is located at the Atlantic entrance to the canal. It is home to some two thousand companies and is

AGRARIAN REFORM IN THE 1970S

Before the 1950s, Panamanian land was available to anyone who wanted to clear and cultivate it. As deforestation increased, the population in these areas rose as people moved onto the cleared land. The amount of farming land available increased, but overplanting depleted the soil. This practice reduced crop yields, and the number of unemployed farmers who could not earn enough by cultivating the land multiplied.

When Omar Torrijos ruled Panama, one of his goals was to reduce poverty and increase employment. Torrijos believed that land, or agrarian, reform would provide the solution. From 1969 to 1977 the government redistributed land and organized farmers into collective agricultural groups. In order to redistribute land, a government commission acquired approximately 1,235,000 acres (500,175 ha) of land and gave individual and collective lots to over eighteen thousand families.

In addition to redistributing land, the commission borrowed a Chilean system that organized farmers into collective agricultural groups. Under this system, the government extended assistance to the peasants within the groups by providing them with credit, training, new roads, wells, and health programs. The government also encouraged the groups to pool land areas and collectively farm the land.

The agrarian reform cost the government a tremendous amount of money, but the incomes of the cooperative farmers remained low. By the late 1970s, the government stressed productivity rather than equity among farmers. Although the reform did not produce the economic results that the government desired, the peasant farmers benefited from the reform in many ways. The new health programs reduced the mortality rate, and the wells gave the farmers greater access to safe drinking water. Training and school programs enabled rural Panamanians to become more educated.

the second largest duty-free zone in the world. The agriculture, forestry, and fishing sectors employ about 17 percent of the workforce, while industry, including manufacturing, mining, and construction, employs 18.6 percent.

Panamanian citizens who are able to work are either employed, unemployed, or "informally employed." The country's city streets are lined with the latter type of employee. They work as street vendors and peddlers and sell handicrafts, market items, and other inexpensive goods on Panama's sidewalks.

During the 1990s Panama became one of the top five countries in Latin America to increase wages and reduce unemployment. Although Panama has the highest GDP per capita in Central America and a growth rate of 5.8 percent, as of 2012, about 26 percent of its population lived in poverty—particularly rural indigenous people. However, that figure shows improvement, as the poverty rate has dropped by 10 percent since 2006.

PROFITS FROM THE LAND AND THE SEA

Before the United States completed the canal, most Panamanians worked on the land. Until the 1950s, the agricultural sector contributed almost 30 percent of the country's GDP. Today agriculture contributes only 3 percent to the GDP. Chief agricultural products are bananas, rice, corn, coffee, sugarcane, vegetables, livestock, and shrimp. Farmers are faced with problems like high labor costs, low levels of mechanization, and the concentration of land ownership in the hands of a few. Many farmers are subsistence farmers, meaning they work to grow enough food to feed themselves and their families, and have little or no surplus to sell.

Panama's chief exports are bananas, shrimp, coffee, raw sugar, and petroleum products. Bananas are the leading export, with annual profits of approximately $220 million. Most bananas are grown in the province of Chiriquí, which is also the site for most of Panama's coffee plantations. Panama exports coffee to the United States, Canada, Saudi Arabia, Germany, Italy, and other European countries.

BANANA BLIGHT

There are hundreds of varieties of bananas in the world—only about half are edible—but most growers in Central and South America grow only one type. Up until the 1950s, all commercially grown bananas were a cultivar called Gros Michel. Then, a deadly blight, first identified in Panama, devastated banana plantations and nearly wiped out the entire variety worldwide. The highly contagious fungus, a type of Fusarium wilt, became known as Panama disease (TR1).

Banana growers switched to a cultivar called the Cavendish, which is the type of banana sold in the United States and Europe today. Although it is supposedly less tasty than the Gros Michel, the Cavendish was thought to be immune to Panama disease.

In the 1990s, however, a new strain of Panama disease (TR4) began spreading across banana plantations in Asia, Africa, and Australia. This fungus does affect the Cavendish variety, as well as many others. Although the disease hasn't shown up yet in the Americas, scientists worry that it's only a matter of time before it does. Since commercial bananas the world over are essentially clones—that is, they are all genetically identical—none of them have natural resistance to the fungus and the world's banana industry is at risk of collapse.

Knowing this, plant breeders are trying to develop a new or hybrid variety of banana that is resistant to the fungus, but which maintains the flavor and other desirable characteristics of today's bananas.

Fishing boats sit in the mud at low tide near Casco Viejo.

FISHING The fishing industry is another area that is important to the economy of Panama. It provides both domestic and international markets with a wide variety of fish from the Atlantic and Pacific Oceans. Many species of fish, as well as lobster and shrimp, are found in Panama's coastal waters. Shrimp is the most profitable and plentiful product, followed by anchovies and herring, which are then processed into food, fish meal, and oil. Most of the shrimp farms are located near Aguadulce on the Pacific coast.

MANUFACTURING

Panama's industries produce cigarettes, alcoholic and carbonated beverages, processed sugar, salt, fish meal and fish oil, and paper products. The manufacturing sector contributes almost 8 percent of the GDP. Over 60 percent of the manufacturing plants are located in Panama City; smaller industrial centers are found in David and Colón.

TRANSPORTATION

Throughout its history, Panama's transportation system has been essential to its economy. The Spanish built the Royal Road in the sixteenth century to transport goods across the isthmus. A few centuries later Panama built its railroad across the isthmus to link the two oceans. Finally, in the early twentieth century, the United States built the canal to facilitate trade.

Besides linking the country's cities to one another, Panama's network of highways and roads also connects it to other countries. Stretching from Alaska to Chile, the Pan-American Highway runs through Panama, and is briefly interrupted in the Darién Gap. The Transístmica, or Trans-Isthmian Highway, links Panama City and Colón. Other highways include the Corredur Sur, a 12-mile (19 km) toll road completed in 2000, to ease the congestion between downtown Panama City and Tocumen International Airport. Until recently, Tocumen was Panama's only international airport, but the new Scarlett Martínez Airport (also known as the Playa Blanca Airport) on the Pacific Coast opened in 2013. There are numerous other airports in Panama that handle domestic flights.

At night, the Corredor Sur glows with the light of traffic traveling in and out of Panama City.

INTERNET LINKS

www.institutionalinvestor.com/Article/3318322/Panamas-Investment-and-Banking-Boom.html#/.V5zTh7grLcs
This 2014 article explains Panama's investment and banking boom.

panamadisease.org
This site provides excellent, easy-to-understand information about bananas and the Panama disease.

ENVIRONMENT

The tiny golden frog, which is really a toad, has become critically endangered in the Panamanian wild.

5

PANAMA IS A RELATIVELY SMALL country, but because of its location, it's environmentally very important. It's a vital link in the Mesoamerican Biological Corridor, the region which connects the ecosystems of North and South America. This unique position makes Panama one of the earth's most biologically diverse nations, and a critical way station for the 122 species of migratory birds that pass through it every year. The country is also home to thousands of endemic plant, tree, and animal species.

Panama faces many challenges in protecting its environment as it deals with increasing population and economic growth. The poor management of natural resources leads to deforestation, pollution, desertification, the loss of natural habitats, and depletion of water resources, as well as the degradation of coastal and marine systems. Long-term environmental degradation often results in problems such as nonpotable or unfiltered drinking water, malnutrition, disease, loss of biodiversity, and soil erosion.

Water pollution from agricultural runoff threatens the country's fisheries, land degradation forces families off their land, and soil erosion increases siltation—when soil and sediments from land are deposited and accumulated in a body of water. Even though Panamanian authorities are working to regulate and enforce legislation regarding deforestation, much still needs to be done to preserve the unique ecosystems and wildlife found in Panama.

DEFORESTATION

About half of Panama's land is forested. Of this, 70 percent is primary forest. Every year, Panama loses about 49,421 acres (20,000 ha) to deforestation, according to the National Association for the Conservation of Nature (ANCON), a Panamanian nonprofit organization. Other estimates are twice that number. Legal and illegal operations and practices such as logging, subsistence farming, and tourism-related development contribute to this loss. Animals lose their habitats and food sources and gradually die out. Indigenous tribes lose their ancestral lands, livelihoods, and knowledge systems of the forest.

Tropical forests help to regulate Panama's ecosystems and the earth's climate. Decomposing leaves and animal matter supply nutrients to the existing vegetation. Trees, in turn, prevent soil erosion. Deforestation cuts off a valuable natural resource that will take a long time to recover.

THE DARIÉN JUNGLE Dense tropical forests cover the country's largest and least inhabited region, the Darién Province. The heavily logged northern Darién has suffered intense environmental damage. Trees are continually felled to make way for new housing, agricultural, and infrastructure projects. Forty years ago, the region north of Yaviza was once covered with virgin forest, but all that remains now are cow pastures.

Loggers, who seek prized Panamanian mahogany for export, build more and more roads to reach deeper into the forest. The timber is sprayed with chemicals to prevent rot and floated down the rivers to the mills, killing fish along the way. Deforestation has led to severe water shortages from Chepo to Yaviza during the dry season and endangered more than thirty native animal species. The paving of the Pan-American Highway to Yaviza has also added to the region's destruction.

The Darién region of Panama, also known as the Darién Gap, is Panama's largest region and has the fewest inhabitants. The Darién Gap extends from east of Panama City and Colón to Colombia. It contains about 12 million acres (5 million ha) of rain forests and swamps. Although this is the largest and one of the most beautiful regions in the country, few Panamanians or tourists visit the Darién Gap because most of the area is accessible only by boat or canoe. For those

who venture on foot into parts of the wilderness, a machete or other strong knife, along with a knowledgeable guide, is needed to penetrate the dense jungle. It is not possible to cross between Panama and Colombia by land without passing through the Darién Gap.

The native Emberá (formerly known as the Chocó) and some Guna people of Panama reside in the dense Darién Gap. The largest concentrations of Emberás and Gunas are found along the coasts of the Sambu and Sabalo Rivers. The longest river in Panama, the Chagres River, runs through the Darién Gap and flows into the Caribbean Sea. The rivers of the Darién serve as highways for the area's residents. The region's abundant flora and fauna also provide food for the Emberás and Gunas.

Human activity threatens to destroy the Darién Gap, one of the most beautiful nature reserves in Central America. The Pan-American Highway that begins in Fairbanks, Alaska, and ends on the southern tip of Chile disappears for 54 miles (87 km) in the Darién Gap. Controversy continues to surround efforts to extend the highway through the rain forest. Already threatened by deforestation, environmental groups fear the highway bisecting the jungle would change the nature of the area for good, and not for the better.

Darién National Park is a UNESCO World Heritage Site for tropical forests, and one of the most important sites in Central America. Despite that, illegal hunting, nomadic settling, and logging persist. The mammoth park is understaffed—not more than twenty rangers are assigned to watch over a staggering 1.4 million acres (579,000 ha) of wilderness.

LAND DEGRADATION

Poverty leads to environmental destruction, which in turn creates even more scarcity. Farmers overexploit thin soils, overgraze fragile grasslands, and cut down trees for firewood. Unsustainable farming practices, such as the slash and burn method, erode the soil and increase siltation in the lakes and waterways feeding the Panama Canal.

A deforested plot quickly becomes infertile and is unable to replenish itself. Such irresponsible land rotations work only in areas with low population densities, and not in places with booming numbers of people who cannot afford to abandon the land. The Sarigua Desert, 150 miles (240 km) southeast of Panama City, shows land degradation at its worst. Years of deforestation, livestock overgrazing, and the loss of topsoil have devastated approximately 19,760 acres (8,000 ha) of land, leaving it utterly barren and saline. Today this wasteland is one of Panama's national parks, one that exhibits the dangers of severe environmental damage.

MANGROVE DEPLETION

Panama has about 170,000 acres (68,795 ha) of mangroves spread along its sea coasts. Three common types of mangroves can be found: the red, black, and white. Mangroves have the unique ability to obtain fresh water from salt water by either excreting excessive salt through their cells or filtering salt out using their roots. They are important in preventing beach erosion, reducing inland flooding during severe storms, and generally maintaining the vital balance in marine ecosystems.

Mangrove root systems preserve water quality and reduce pollution by filtering out suspended materials. They also provide habitat, shelter, and food for many animals. Many water birds, such as the brown pelican, white ibis, and great blue heron, rely on mangroves for nesting.

Unfortunately, large swathes of mangroves are being cleared to make room for shrimp farms, resorts, and urban development. The loss of these wetlands, including swamps, has drastically reduced the number of reservoirs and rain catchments. When these areas become degraded or depleted, the government will have to invest in expensive treatment plants, dams, and other flood-control measures.

Mangroves grow in the sheltered lagoon coasts of the Bocas del Toro region on the Caribbean coast.

ENDANGERED SPECIES

According to the World Conservation Monitoring Center, Panama has 1,569 known species of amphibians, birds, mammals, and reptiles. Of these, 6 percent, including the golden frog, are threatened with extinction. Others include sea turtles, the ornate spider monkey, the jaguar, and the harpy eagle.

The harpy eagle is one of the largest eagles in the world. It inhabits primary tropical and subtropical forests, and can be found in places with elevations up to 5,250 feet (1,600 m). This bird species requires at least 7 square miles (18 square km) of forest to thrive and raise its offspring. Logging, poaching, and agricultural development have substantially reduced the number of habitats. It is difficult to protect the harpy eagle from poachers because its habitats are so remote and inaccessible.

PROTECTED AREAS

About one-quarter of Panama's land lies within its seventy-six protected areas. There are fifteen national parks, twelve forest reserves, and ten wildlife sanctuaries. Soberanía National Park, for example, is a secondary tropical forest. Its 55,000 acres (22,257 ha) are home to some 525 species of birds, more than 100 species of mammals, 80 kinds of reptiles, and 55 types of amphibians. However, formal protection and law-enforcement mechanisms are still lacking. Soberanía is experiencing severe deforestation and hunting incursions as settlements increase along its northeastern boundary. Its accessibility and proximity to Panama City (just 30 minutes away) means that population growth and expanding development pose a constant threat.

Spanning roughly 300,000 acres (121,403 ha), Chagres National Park's rich cloud forests provide a ready source of fresh water for the Panama Canal. It, too, hosts an abundance of plant and animal species. The seven thousand people living inside the park, together with the twenty-five thousand residing around the river basin, exert added pressure on the area's natural resources.

Forested areas that are under protection include the canal watershed, San Lorenzo, the Bocas del Toro region, the northern province of Chiriquí, and the Guna Yala comarca region. Other areas include Coiba, an island in the Pacific, and Barro Colorado Island, which is home to one of the world's leading research centers, the Smithsonian Tropical Research Institute.

ENERGY

With its many rivers, Panama has traditionally relied on hydroelectric power as a source of energy. About 54 percent of Panama's energy comes from hydro sources—there are nine hydropower stations in operation and reportedly another thirty-seven are in the planning, design, or construction phase. Since Panama does not produce any crude oil, natural gas, or coal, it has to rely completely on imports of fossil fuels, which supply about 44 percent of the country's energy. There are no nuclear power plants in the country.

The newly built Barro Blanco Dam has been a subject of much controversy. The dam on the Tabasara River is expected to provide an additional 29 megawatts of much-needed energy to Panama's supply. However, the massive project borders a community of Ngöbe-Buglé people, who insist that the dam and its reservoir will irreparably destroy their way of life. This dispute has caused long delays in the opening of the power plant.

Although Panama doesn't produce fossil fuels, it serves as a critical conduit for international transportation of natural gas and crude oil. The newly enlarged canal can now accommodate large tankers carrying natural gas that were previously forced to sail around Cape Horn. The Trans-Panama Pipeline, an oil pipeline that runs between Charco Azul Bay on the Atlantic coast and Chiriquí Grande terminal along Panama's Pacific coast, is another important transportation system.

INTERNET LINKS

www.anywherepanama.com/travel-guide/environmental-issues
This is a good overview of Panama's major environmental challenges. The site itself has links to very informative pages about all of Panama's regions, national parks, along with excellent photos and maps.

www.coha.org/cementing-its-legacy-the-panamanian-governments-damning-of-the-ngabe-bugle
This article describes the conflict between the Panamanian government and the Ngöbe-Buglé people over the construction of the Barro Blanco Dam.

www.reuters.com/article/us-panama-deforestation-idUSKCN0YOOBT
This 2016 article explains how Panama's indigenous people are using drones to monitor deforestation.

www.outsideonline.com/1903361/impossible-place-be
This long but fascinating firsthand account of one reporter's excursion into the Darién Gap jungle includes good information about deforestation.

whc.unesco.org/en/list/159
The World Heritage entry for the Darién National Park provides a wealth of environmental information about the site along with some photos.

PANAMANIANS

A Guna woman wears traditional clothing and makeup in Playon Chico, Panama.

6

LIKE MOST COUNTRIES IN THE Americas, Panama is home to a diverse population. Panamanians hail from several different ethnic groups. Panamanian mestizos (may-STEE-zos) are the descendants of a mixture of indigenous and European ancestry. Approximately 65 percent of the approximately 3,657,000 people in Panama are mestizos, and another 6.8 percent are mulattoes, those who have mixed European and African heritage. Another 9.2 percent are Afro-Caribbean, 12.3 percent are Native Americans, and the remaining 6.7 percent are white.

Naturally, not everyone fits neatly into one of these categories, as people of various races and ethnicities have mixed over the centuries. Panamanians form a highly diverse society as they are descended from native peoples and immigrants from all over the world.

Panama has become a popular place for expats from the United States to live. The US State Department estimates that some fourteen thousand US citizens are living in Panama. Many have moved there because of its affordability, pleasant climate, dollarized economy, widely spoken English, and excellent retirement benefits.

Ethnicity is an important social distinction in Panama, yet the Panamanian subcultures have merged to the point that it is now difficult to distinguish individuals as belonging to a particular ethnic group. Nonetheless, Panamanians classify themselves into three principal groups—the Roman Catholic mestizos who speak Spanish, the Protestant Afro-Caribbeans, many of whom speak a Panamanian English Creole—a mix of English and Spanish—and the indigenous natives.

The mestizos and Afro-Caribbeans reside in both the cities and the rural areas. The majority of the indigenous peoples live in the more remote regions such as Guna Yala (the province in northeast Panama that includes the San Blas Islands) and the Darién region. The Panamanians of foreign descent reside primarily in the larger cities.

INDIGENOUS PEOPLE

Historians say approximately half a million to eight hundred thousand people of more than sixty tribal groups lived in Panama before the Europeans arrived in the sixteenth century. When the Spaniards arrived they conquered the groups and enslaved, tortured, and killed the indigenous peoples. Many who survived the brutality died after contracting diseases that the Spaniards brought with them. To escape the massacres and diseases, thousands of indigenous peoples fled to the remote areas of Panama where they still live.

Today there are seven indigenous groups in Panama: the Guna, Emberá, Ngöbe (NAH-bay), Wounaan, Buglé (boo-GLAY), Naso, and Bribri. The three largest groups are the Guna, Emberá, and Ngöbe-Buglé. The Buglé people have common territorial ancestry with the Ngöbe group, but the two groups speak different languages.

The smaller groups include the Bribri, who live near Costa Rica, the Bókata in eastern Bocas del Toro, and the Naso, who live along the Teribe River. They are under the jurisdiction of the national and provincial governments, but many groups remain virtually autonomous, each with its own distinct language and culture. The indigenous groups have largely organized themselves into five divisions along political and territorial lines called *comarcas*.

Most Guna (previously spelled Kuna or Cuna) people live in the Archípíelago de San Blás (the San Blas Islands) and the mainland section of the Comarca de Guna Yala. Although they were the largest group before the Spaniards arrived, the Gunas constitute only 20 percent of the indigenous population today. The Gunas, more than any other group, have retained their cultural heritage. They have resisted Spanish influence and live very much the same way the Spaniards found them in the early sixteenth century.

The Emberás populate villages within the Darién jungle. Formerly known as the Chocós because they emigrated from the Chocó province of Colombia during the late eighteenth century, they live much like their ancestors did—hunting and gathering, and collecting forest plants for medicinal purposes. Certain customs are still widely practiced, such as painting bodies with plant dyes and using poisoned blowgun darts for hunting. The Emberás are also renowned for their intricate handicrafts. Woven baskets, distinctive pottery, and carved figurines of animals are sold throughout Panama. These works of traditional art fetch high prices when they are exported to North America. However, widespread deforestation and aggressive farming techniques are threatening the Emberá way of life. Many individuals have started cultivating

A band of Emberá men and boys play music for tourists.

A woman walks on a mountain slope in the Chiriquí region.

cash crops in order to support their families.

The Ngöbe-Buglés, who account for 68 percent of the indigenous population, are located in the mountainous regions of Chiriquí, Veraguas, and Bocas del Toro. They live in hamlets, with as many as three generations of family members and relatives under one roof. A person's social identity and individual roles within the hamlet are well defined. They rely on crop raising, hunting, fishing, and livestock production for their livelihood.

SOCIAL SYSTEM

Panama's social system is made up of three tiers—the elite, the middle class, and the lower class. The class structure divides citizens based on wealth, occupation, education, family background, culture, and race.

Panama's social system began in Spanish colonial times and has continued until today. The Spanish military and colonists exploited the Natives, conquering their lands and enslaving and killing them. The Spanish also brought African slaves to Panama and the Caribbean. (During the building of the Panama Canal a century ago, thousands of workers came from Barbados, Jamaica, and Trinidad. Some of today's black Panamanians are descended from them.) The native peoples and Africans made up the lower levels of society. The middle class emerged when people moved out of the settlement areas and formed smaller societies. This class usually did not use slaves, and because they did their own work, the elite class looked down on them.

THE ELITE Wealth, power, and prestige are highly concentrated in the hands of the Panamanian elite living in the cities. They traditionally consist of wealthy families descended from colonial times, and *nouveau riche* immigrants, who have become part of this social class through business or marriage. Mostly of white European descent, they are called *rabiblancos* or "whitetails," a disparaging term. Presidents, cabinet officials, and governors have come from this class. Elite status is usually acquired through birth and breeding; however, some Panamanians have improved their status through education. Education is considered to be a mark of the elite and a vast majority of those in this class are university graduates. Panamanians view a profession, such as law or medicine, as a status symbol and as a gateway to the political arena.

THE MIDDLE CLASS About a quarter of the population enjoys a middle-class standard of living. They usually reside in Panama City. Some, however, run rural businesses in small towns. Mestizos dominate the middle class. Some Afro-Caribbeans have moved into this class, as have descendants of the railroad workers and immigrants from other countries. Many are working professionals who send their children to local universities.

THE LOWER CLASS Most rural and indigenous Panamanians belong to the lower class. In the countryside, people struggle to survive and many leave in search of a better life in the cities. These migrants find work in the cities as semi-skilled laborers and domestic workers. Over the past few decades, however, some ethnic groups have become more educated and wealthy, and have moved up the social ladder. Some Afro-Caribbeans, for example, have moved from their laborer status to higher positions in Panamanian society. Education has been the key to their advancement in the social hierarchy. Nevertheless, most black Panamanians are among the country's poorest, most discriminated-against people.

CLOTHING

Panamanians are fairly conservative and formal in their dress. Within the city, businessmen often dress less formally than their American counterparts. For instance, men often wear a cotton shirt called a *guayabera*, which is a loose-fitting, short-sleeved cotton shirt that is not tucked into the trousers. In some professions, such as banking and law, men and women wear lightweight suits.

Young women wear brightly colored polleras at a festive celebration.

Panamanians frown on people wearing shorts in public, no matter how hot the weather is. Men may occasionally wear shorts, but society considers it inappropriate for women to wear shorts or trousers in public. Although Panamanians grant leniency to tourists who wear shorts, they prefer that foreigners abide by their somewhat stringent dress code.

TRADITIONAL CLOTHING FOR WOMEN The national dress for women is the *pollera* (poh-YEH-rah), a long, full dress made from white cotton. Brightly colored embroidery adorns the beautiful dress, and the women wear it for national celebrations, carnivals, and special occasions. The *peineta* (peh-ee-NEH-tah) is the headpiece that the women wear with the pollera. The peineta consists of veils and large, elaborate combs with dangling ornaments.

The *pollera de gala* (poh-YEH-rah de GAH-lah) is the "deluxe" version of the pollera and consists of several intricately embroidered petticoats under a full, embroidered skirt. The petticoats and the skirt are made of fine material and lace, and the embroidery, called *aderozo* (ah-deh-ROH-soh), is colorful. The off-shoulder blouse also has intricate embroidery.

Guna women also have a traditional dress that consists of a blue printed wraparound skirt, gold rings in both the nose and ears, strings of yellow and red beads around the arms and legs, a black line painted on the nose, and a blouse with *mola* (MOH-lah) panels. A mola is a panel created by reverse appliquéing brightly colored cloth behind a black fabric background. Typically, a blouse will have one mola on the front and another on the back. Guna women's attire varies based on their marital status, and an unmarried woman wears her hair long, while a married woman cuts hers short.

TRADITIONAL CLOTHING FOR MEN The traditional clothing for Panamanian men is the *montuno* (mohn-TOO-noh). The montuno consists of a white cotton embroidered shirt and short trousers. As part of this traditional garb, men often wear a straw hat called a *pintado* (pin-TAH-doh). This hat has a distinctive curled-up brim and black patches on it. The men also wear sandals with this outfit.

INTERNET LINKS

www.anywherepanama.com/travel-guide/people-and-culture
This Panama travel site has information on the people of Panama.

www.famousbirthdays.com/birthplace/panama.html
Well-known Panamanians and Panamanian-Americans are profiled on this site.

minorityrights.org/minorities/afro-panamanians
This organization offers a world directory of minorities and indigenous people. This page provides an overview of Afro-Panamanians. There are links to pages for Chinese Panamanians, Guaymi, and Kuna (Guna) minorities as well.

www.thelovelyplanet.net/traditional-dress-of-panama-the-exotic-mola-and-la-pollera
This site shows beautiful photos of traditional Panamanian clothing.

LIFESTYLE

An indigenous man makes a dugout canoe as a boy looks on and helps.

7

A PANAMANIAN'S DAY-TO-DAY lifestyle is hard to generalize because the people themselves are so different. The lifestyle of a middle-class businessman in Panama City is worlds away from that of a Guna woman living on an island off the Caribbean coast or an Emberá boy living deep in the jungle of the Darién region. But one thing all Panamanians have in common is the importance that they place on family. Panamanians consider their family to be their support, their responsibility, and the ultimate recipient of their loyalty. Panamanians frequently visit their family members, even after marriage. Besides strong family ties, Panamanians also value friendships and interact with their friends in the same way as their American counterparts.

In Panama, the school year runs from February to December and is divided into three semesters.

A tidy bedroom inside a basic Guna bamboo hut on Isla Pelikano, one of the San Blas islands

Social gatherings in Panama have certain customs that guests follow. For instance, guests at large social gatherings introduce themselves to other guests and do not expect the host or hostess to introduce them. Guests don't feel compelled to arrive on time. Even if the party begins at 10 p.m., Panamanians consider arriving two hours late as an acceptable practice. At a smaller party, however, etiquette suggests that a guest should not arrive later than a half hour after the starting time. Regardless of the scale of the party, a Panamanian host or hostess appreciates a small gift from each guest.

FAMILY LIFE

Panamanians are very loyal to their families and have historically viewed their family ties as a defense against an uncertain and hostile world. Often, Panamanians are more loyal to their parents and siblings than to their spouses. In many Panamanian families, particularly those in rural areas, it is common to find three generations living under one roof. Family members steadfastly come to one another's aid if needed, and support one another throughout life.

FAMILY LIFE FOR THE GUNA PEOPLE The Gunas live mainly on the San Blas Islands or in the Darién region. They consider the family the most important unit, and many members of one family will live in a single hut. Men dominate Guna society, and the most senior man in a hut is the head of the household. When a daughter marries, her husband comes to live with her family, and the husband is subordinate to her father. The son-in-law often tries to establish his own household after a few years.

Labor in the Guna household is traditionally divided. The men hunt and gather food, while the women perform the household duties and sew for the family. In their spare time, they make molas. The women inherit the land that they live on from their fathers. Therefore, parents usually hope for girls.

FAMILY LIFE FOR THE NGÖBE-BUGLÉ PEOPLE Ngöbe-Buglé people, also known as the Guaymi, are actually two separate groups with completely different languages that share the same region. The Ngöbe are the more populous of the two. Both groups live in hamlets, with many family members and relatives residing within the same settlement. The hamlets are scattered throughout the mountainous Ngöbe-Buglé comarca but don't form villages or towns. A couple can live either with the husband's family or the wife's family.

This group also has clearly defined roles for men and women. For instance, the women do not clear the forest, hunt, or herd cattle, but they chop firewood. The men usually do not care for the children, cook, or clean. The children begin to help their parents with the chores when they are eight years old, and their parents expect them to do the work of an adult by the time girls turn fourteen years old, and boys reach seventeen years old. Few children attend school past the sixth grade.

FAMILY LIFE FOR THE EMBERÁ The Emberás are a much smaller group as compared to the Gunas or Ngöbe-Buglés. They live deep within the Darién jungle in small groups of one or two extended families. Over the past few decades, the Panamanian government has encouraged the Emberá to establish settled communities and attend schools within villages. Many now live in cinderblock houses rather than the old-style dwellings. These are open-air homes on platforms raised 12 to 16 feet (4 m to 5 m) above the ground. They traditionally have roofs made of thatched palm leaves and floors made of palm bark, but these days are more likely to have aluminum roofing and wooden floors. Many Emberá have even moved to the cities. According to the 2010 Panamanian National Census, more than 25 percent of the Panamanian Emberá population resides in urban districts of Panama City.

MARRIAGE

The majority of Panamanian men and women choose their own spouses. Couples, particularly from the rural middle and lower classes, often decide to marry and have children together, but do not participate in a formal marriage ceremony until years later. In fact, the children often encourage their parents' formal marriage. If the union between these unmarried couples does not work out, the children usually stay with their mothers.

Many Panamanians, especially from the elite and middle classes, choose to participate in a formal marriage ceremony before starting a life with another person. Among these classes, marriage plays an integral role in maintaining or improving a family's social status. Although the families do not arrange the marriages, they encourage their children to marry individuals of wealth and similar ancestry.

Marriage also plays an important role among the Native groups in Panama. In order to maintain their racial purity, the Guna do not marry outside the group. The Ngöbe-Buglé

An elegant bride looks out over the sea.

view marriage as the most important event in a person's life. Fathers usually arrange their children's marriages based on the selected spouse's land, wealth, and position in the group. Some Ngöbe-Buglé men practice polygamy, or marriage to more than one woman. An older man sometimes marries his wife's younger sister, and the wives raise their children together.

BIRTH

Most Panamanians desire children and celebrate their birth. While some opt not to marry or have babies, the overwhelming majority of Panamanians still hope for children.

A couple will take great care in choosing godparents for their child. Most Panamanians believe that the godparents play a vital role in the child's life, thus the selection process is an important one.

The Guna typically have large families, and a couple hopes for a girl so that when she marries, she will bring a son-in-law into the family.

Life for Panamanian infants can be difficult in some regions. Many face malnutrition and inadequate medical care, and these problems are most severe among rural indigenous groups. Malnutrition is usually caused by poverty. One out of four children suffer from some degree of malnutrition, and infants in the rural areas are three times more likely to be malnourished than their city counterparts. Chronic malnutrition in children between six and nine years old is estimated to affect 68 percent of the indigenous population and 42 percent of those in the poorest districts. Unfortunately, many Panamanian parents are often too poor to provide adequate food for their offspring.

MEN AND WOMEN

Over the past few decades the roles of Panamanian men and women have changed. Although most females still do not enjoy the same economic, social, and educational opportunities as the men, women's opportunities have improved. Today, more Panamanian women have access to secondary and upper-level education. Women are also entering fields that were traditionally male-dominated, such as medicine, banking, and law.

In an Emberá village, a woman holds her baby son.

Traditionally, Panamanian men and women have clearly defined roles in society. Parents send their sons to better schools and give them more freedom than their daughters. Men dominate not only the workplace, but the home as well.

In rural society, men and women also have gender-specific roles. The men work outside of the home farming and raising crops or animals, while the women remain at home caring for the children. Many rural women are illiterate, because education for females is a low priority in the lifestyle and minds of peasant families.

Panama's Native groups have similar societal roles for men and women, with both genders adhering to the traditional division of labor. Guna men hunt and fish, while the women are confined to the performance of domestic chores as wives and mothers. Women typically do not leave the settlement, but the men will often leave for years and go to college. In the Ngöbe-Buglé group, women have a subservient role to men and often have to share their husband with other women.

The Emberá group, however, elevates women to a more equal status in their society. Females work in the fields and have property rights. Even though the Emberá society is patrilineal, meaning that the children in a family inherit from their father rather than their mother, the men still respect the women and include them in making important decisions.

CHILDREN

Despite the emerging trend of more women working outside the home, children spend most of their early years with their mothers. In the rural areas, children often live with their parents until they marry; sometimes they continue living with a spouse's parents even after marriage. In the cities, children either remain with their parents until marriage or live on their own in apartments when they become young adults.

Children are also very important to the native groups. Guna couples bear many children, and the mother takes on the nurturing role. Male children do not wear clothes until they are between five and seven years old. Female children, however, begin wearing the native dresses with molas when they are born. When an infant girl is one month old, the Gunas pierce her nose and insert a coconut-soaked thread. After a few days her mother puts a nose ring through the hole, and the child continues to wear larger rings as she grows up.

EDUCATION

Panamanian law requires that children from seven to fifteen years old attend school, and education during these years is provided free of charge by the government. Children, however, do not always attend school due to traditional attitudes, financial problems, lack of transportation, and lack of

LIFE IN THE DARIÉN GAP

In the Darién region, several indigenous groups, such as the Emberá, live amid the dense foliage of the jungle. Settlements are dotted along the twisting rivers and mountains.

Life in the Darién jungle is neither luxurious nor easy. The residents battle extreme heat, wild animals, and swarms of mosquitoes. Although the rivers serve as their principal means of transportation, it's difficult to navigate through tangled vines and trees. The Darién's inhabitants rely upon the region's plants and animals for food and resources, but occasionally venture out to acquire modern goods. They build their homes from trees, sticks, grass, and leaves.

The people are friendly to the occasional visitor, but they resist adopting modern ways. The Emberás are skilled artisans who make beautiful baskets, carvings, and necklaces, but they prefer to exchange these products for blue jeans, sneakers, flashlights, or nylon windbreakers instead of selling them to visitors.

government enforcement. The problem is most extreme in Darién Province and among indigenous groups.

Panama's quality of education has increased dramatically during the past century. In 1923, over 70 percent of Panamanians were illiterate; today only 5 percent cannot read. Panama's education system is divided into three levels: primary school (six years), secondary school (six years), and university or higher education. Primary school enrollment is high, at more than 90 percent.

Panama has eighty-eight institutes of higher education, including smaller colleges and three main universities. Many are located in Panama City, and many are affiliated with universities in the United States or Canada. The state-run University of Panama, the Technological University, and the private Catholic University of Santa María La Antigua are some of the top schools. To attend a university, a student must complete the upper cycle of secondary school and acquire a *bachillerato* (bah-chee-yay-RAH-toh), or diploma. Out of every three eligible candidates, only one will secure a place. The university program lasts six years.

An albino Guna student studies at a computer in a high school in Nargana, Panama. Albinism is a condition in which a person lacks melanin, which forms pigmentation in eyes, hair, and skin. The Guna have a high incidence of albinism.

HEALTH AND WELFARE

The people of Panama enjoy some of the best health care in Latin America. Males born in 2015 could expect to live 75.7 years, on average, and females, 81.4 years. Panamanians have enjoyed higher health standards since the government took charge of the health-care system in the 1970s and elected a minister to oversee public health in the late 1980s. Rural health care has improved significantly. However, there is still a disparity in standards between rural and urban health care, because advanced medical facilities are concentrated in the cities. Clinics that are located in rural areas are difficult to reach and often lack high-tech equipment and varieties of medicine.

Panama's government allotted nearly $2 billion to health care in 2015, some of which was earmarked for the construction of new facilities in rural areas. The Ministry of Health employs medical directors to maintain health-care services, manage hospitals, operate health centers, and spearhead related programs at the district and regional levels. The Social Security Institute provides retirement pensions and health care for its members.

A street in a poorer section of downtown Colón

URBAN LIFE

Over the past half century, Panamanians have moved to the cities in droves. Until the 1950s only one-third of Panama's population was urban. By 2015, two-thirds of the people—some 66 percent—were living in the cities. The rate of extreme poverty in urban areas is only 4 percent, compared to about 27 percent in rural areas.

The presence of the Panama Canal has encouraged many rural folks to move to the cities. Two of the country's largest cities, Panama City and Colón, are located on the canal. When combined, they house over two-thirds of Panama's urban population.

Panamanian city dwellers live in houses or apartment buildings made of wood or concrete. The wealthier residents live in grand old colonial houses, while the middle class live in more moderate homes or apartments. The less affluent residents live in cramped slum communities with thousands of others.

Historically, city dwellers isolated themselves based on wealth, race, and social status. Before the influx of rural migrants over the past few decades, cities were somewhat segregated based on these indicators. Today urban

sprawl has blurred the distinctions. Although upper-class city areas still exist, it is now more common to have different social classes living in the same neighborhood.

RURAL LIFE

The majority of rural residents are poor—especially in indigenous territories. In those regions, about 70 percent of people live in poverty, including 40 percent who are in extreme poverty. Rural people are far more likely to live without access to sanitation, clean water, and in some cases, electricity. There is also a strong correlation between poverty and malnutrition. The Food and Agriculture Organization of the United Nations (FAO) reported in 2015 that chronic malnutrition in children from indigenous regions of Panama is greater than 19 percent, well ahead of the Latin American average, which is 12.8 percent.

Although rural life is more primitive than urban life, the Panamanian government has instituted several health and welfare programs to benefit the rural communities. Many villages and towns now enjoy more advanced health care and access to clean water. The Torrijos government also established collectives and redistributed rural farmland. Many Panamanians who acquired land through this program, however, sold it to wealthy cattle ranchers and migrated to the cities.

INTERNET LINKS

www.anywherepanama.com/travel-guide/crime-and-safety
Issues of crime and safety throughout Panama are addressed here.

www.anywherepanama.com/travel-guide/people-and-culture
This site takes a look at some of the cultural norms of daily life in Panama.

www.humanium.org/en/americas/panama
This children's rights organization provides an overview of the situation for children in Panama.

www.intltravelnews.com/2012/02/look-life-panama%E2%80%99s-ember%C3%A1-tribe
This travel article describes a visit to an Emberá village.

www.worldbank.org/en/country/panama/overview
The World Bank gives an overview of poverty reduction efforts in Panama.

RELIGION

A rusty cross in Colón overlooks the entrance to the Panama Canal.

8

RELIGIOUS FREEDOM IS GUARANTEED by the Panamanian constitution. The country's larger cities, in particular, have a diversity of faith communities. For example, in addition to Christian churches, Panama City also has synagogues, mosques, one of the world's eight Baha'i Houses of Worship, and the Greek Orthodox Metropolitanate of Central America.

Nevertheless, like all of Latin America, Panama is largely Roman Catholic. Exact numbers are uncertain because the Panamanian government doesn't collect census statistics on the religious affiliation of its citizens. However, it is generally acknowledged that about 75 to 85 percent of Panamanians are Roman Catholics; some 15 percent are evangelical Protestants; and the rest are Jews, Muslims, Baha'is, Hindus, or not affiliated with a particular faith. Panama's indigenous peoples follow their own religions, or in some cases, combine them with Catholicism. A survey published by the Pew Research Center in 2014 found that 66 percent of Panamanian Catholics and 46 percent of Protestants engage in at least three out of the eight indigenous beliefs and practices.

The Spaniards established the Catholic faith as Panama's main religion in the sixteenth century, and Panamanians have embraced

Christmas and Easter are the two most important religious holidays for Panamanian Catholics. Another important day is the Feast of the Immaculate Conception on December 8, which Panamanians also celebrate as Mother's Day. On this day, Catholics honor both the Virgin Mary and their own mothers.

Catholicism since then. Devout Catholics visit the church and observe religious duties daily, while the less devout, or liberal, Catholics adhere to the religious calendar.

In 2016, Pope Francis announced that Panama City is set to host the Catholic Church's 2019 World Youth Day, an international event for young people that occurs every three years. It will be the first World Youth Day to take place in Central America since the event's beginning in 1986.

THE CONSTITUTION AND RELIGION

Panama's constitution provides for freedom of religion, meaning that citizens may follow any faith—or none at all—without the government's interference. A citizen may not be punished for professing an unusual religion or forming a new one. The constitution also prohibits the government from discriminating against religious groups. Each religion is entitled to equal protection under the law.

Panama does not have a state religion, but Roman Catholicism is the predominant faith. The constitution states that schools may, but do not have to, instruct students on Roman Catholicism. Panama's constitution, unlike the US Constitution, does not require or call for separation of church and state.

The constitution prohibits members of the clergy from holding public office in the country, unless the office relates to social assistance, education, or scientific research. It requires senior officials within the church hierarchy to be native-born Panamanians. The constitution allows foreign clergy who enter Panama to enjoy the same religious freedoms as Panamanian citizens. This means that, unlike other members of the clergy who are Panamanian citizens, foreign clergy may hold public office, but cannot be senior members of the church.

ROMAN CATHOLICISM

The Spanish were the first European settlers in Panama, and they introduced the Roman Catholic religion to Panama. Pedro Arias Dávila, or Pedrarias

the Cruel, organized Panama's Catholic religion according to the laws of the church. He thwarted the native groups' rebellions and tried to convert the various indigenous groups to Christianity.

At the end of the eighteenth century, the Roman Catholic Church established the first bishopric, or office of bishop, on the American continent in Panama City. Unfortunately during his rampage in 1671, Henry Morgan destroyed the cathedral that housed the first American diocese. Panama has followed the Spanish version of Roman Catholicism for almost four hundred years. By the time Panama declared its independence from Spain, Roman Catholicism had been deeply ingrained in the people, and remains the most popular religion among Panamanians today.

CATHOLIC RITUALS AND BELIEFS According to Christians, Jesus Christ established a church that was to encompass all races, cultures, and nations. He called this church "catholic," meaning "universal" or "all-embracing." Catholics believe that popes, bishops, and priests are the successors of Jesus's apostles and are placed on earth to spread the word of God.

A white statue of Christ gleams against the blue sky in a park in Colón.

The statue of the Black Christ is bedecked with a sumptuous robe in the Iglesia de San Felipe in Portobelo.

God's word to Christians is represented through the Bible. The Old Testament of the Bible tells the story of God forming the Old Covenant with the Hebrew people. The New Testament tells the story of God's work through his son, Jesus Christ. Catholics believe in the Holy Trinity, the concept that there is one God, existing as three "persons"—God the Father, the Son, and the Holy Spirit. Jesus Christ, therefore, is understood as both human and God. Catholics also believe that the pope, the leader of the worldwide Catholic Church, is the successor to Saint Peter, and derives his authority directly from God.

In sixteenth-century Europe, the Protestant Reformation drew many believers away from the Catholic Church. However, since its colonizer, Spain, was a Catholic nation, Panama remained a Catholic country as well.

Panamanian Catholics have many religious beliefs that are exclusive to their country. For instance, Catholics from all over the country worship the Black Christ, whose life-size wooden sculpture is housed in an eighteenth-century church in Portobelo. Every October 21, hundreds of worshippers visit the statue. Many worshippers wear purple garments like the ones that adorn the statue. In order to atone for their sins, some believers dress in purple robes and crawl on the road as an act of penance. Some devout worshippers attach gold charms to their garments as symbols of faith.

CATHEDRALS

Panama is home to many beautiful places of worship, and many churches were built during the Spanish colonial days. The country also has places of worship for Protestants, Muslims, Hindus, and Baha'is. Panama's oldest church is located in Nata, a town along the Gulf of Panama. The Spaniards built this church in 1520, and Catholics still worship at this beautiful old church today.

When the buccaneer, Henry Morgan, attacked the old Panama City, he destroyed many beautiful churches, and most of the city. The cathedral was burned, but an imposing belfry tower and some walls still remain. Morgan and his men demolished many buildings and stole countless gold and priceless items during his rampage through Panama. Legend has it that the magnificent Altar de Oro ("Golden Altar") in one of the churches was spared when a priest painted it black and convinced the pirates that it had already been stolen.

The Metropolitan Cathedral in Casco Viejo is a major tourist attraction.

After the raiders left town, the altar was reinstated in a new cathedral, the Inglesia de San Jose (Church of San Jose), built in 1671. Today that church and its famous altar, now restored, is a tourist attraction in Casco Viejo, the historic section of Panama City.

The Metropolitan Cathedral is Panama City's largest cathedral. Many interesting events have occurred at this site. When Omar Torrijos died, the viewing of his body and his funeral were held here. In 1990, President Guillermo Endara fasted at the church for almost two weeks to protest the lack of American financial aid following their 1989 invasion to overthrow Noriega. Besides spurring the United States to action, the president also wanted to show Panama's poor that he understood the situations that they were facing.

INDIGENOUS BELIEFS

THE GUNAS Although some Gunas practice the Catholic faith, the majority retain ancestral indigenous beliefs. Ritual plays an important role in the Guna faith, and members of the group gain prestige through their knowledge of the rituals.

An important Guna ritual is the *inna-nega* (een-NAH nay-GAH), or "coming-out" party, for young women. When a girl reaches puberty, the tribe

A young girl's coming-of-age party is decorated with balloons in a Guna community in the Guna Yala region.

holds a three-day celebration. Before the ritual, the young woman's female relatives decide on a special mola that they will all wear. These women secretly make the molas, which may become popular throughout the Guna region that year. During the first two days of the celebration, the women serve food and drink. The *kantules* (kahn-TOO-lays), or priests, sit in a ceremonial house, and the group chants stories about the history of the Gunas. On the third day, the women join in and the group bestows a permanent name upon the young woman and cuts her hair.

The Gunas believe that they enter another life after death. To achieve honor in the next life, they strive to reach a high level in their current life. One way to achieve a high status is to collect the teeth of the white-faced monkey, a fierce animal. The Gunas kill the monkey and put its teeth on a necklace. The more monkeys a Guna kills, the longer the necklace. The Gunas believe that they will be rewarded in their next life if they had a long necklace of monkey teeth during their lifetime on Earth.

THE EMBERÁS The Emberá people, despite visits from religious missionaries, continue to worship their own gods. The men carve ritual sculptures and altars dedicated to their gods. When Emberás are sick, they try to cure themselves first with medicinal plants. If this treatment is unsuccessful, they seek the help of one of the group's *jabaina* (ha-bah-EE-nah), or medicine men, who calls upon the gods for assistance.

Emberá men usually wear only a loin cloth that is held up by a string tied around their waists. For religious ceremonies and other festivities, the men wear multicolored woven pants, a beaded chest plate, and hammered silver crowns, earrings, and bracelets. From their ankles to their lower lips, Emberás paint themselves with a black pigment extracted from the seeds of a local fruit. They apply the pigment in elaborate patterns, which lasts for about ten days.

The Emberá women, who usually wear dresses or other suitable clothes for the warm weather, also have a special costume for religious events. They tie a brilliantly colored cloth around their hips, and it extends to their knees, similar to a skirt. They usually do not wear a shirt or blouse for these events and are bare-chested except for beaded necklaces. The women also decorate their skin with black pigment.

Clad in a traditional loin cloth, an Emberá man plays a flute.

THE NGÖBE-BUGLÉ Another Native group, the Ngöbe-Buglé people, also have their own religious beliefs. The Spanish colonists found the Ngöbe-Buglés to be fierce warriors and tried to group them into settlements controlled by a Roman Catholic missionary. Some Ngöbe-Buglés converted to Christianity, but most of them rebelled against the Spanish control and moved to remote areas of the country.

The Ngöbe-Buglé religion is ritualistic, and music and celebrations are very important. The Ngöbe-Buglés make their own instruments out of animal bones, large seashells, turtle shells, wood, and animal skins. During religious events and other festivities, men and women paint different designs on their faces and file their incisor teeth into sharp points, which resemble fangs.

One of the most important rituals is the *guro* (GOO-roh), which occurs when a boy reaches puberty. Unlike the Guna inna-nega, the guro is a mysterious ritual in which only the men participate. The elders of the group take the young man into the jungle and make him complete difficult physical tests to prove his endurance. The elders chant as the young man undergoes the tests.

The Ngöbe-Buglé religion permits polygamy, and some of the men have several wives. However, people who have converted to Christianity are monogamous, and polygamy is no longer common.

FOLK BELIEFS

Rural Panamanians have unique folk beliefs. Although many rural Panamanians are Roman Catholics, their folk beliefs have been so deeply integrated with their religious beliefs that they practice a hybrid form of Catholicism. The folklore places God, the devil, the Virgin Mary, and saints at the center of the belief system. The believers view Jesus Christ as the chief saint, but do not centralize him as the Catholic faith does. Women admire the Virgin Mary, and try to emulate her actions and beliefs.

A statue of the Virgin Mary and the Christ Child adorns a shrine.

ALL SOULS' DAY To rural Panamanians, the devil represents the evil that can alter their destiny, which is set by God. According to folklore, the devil constantly entices humans to live in condemnation with him in the afterlife by offering them almost irresistible things on earth. When a person dies, Saint Peter will use a balance scale to weigh the person's good and bad deeds. If the good deeds outweigh the bad, the person will spend the afterlife in heaven. If not, the person will go to hell. The weighing process occurs annually on All Souls' Day, when God and the devil summon those who died in the previous year before them. The living, however, spend All Souls' Day reviewing their own lives. Even urban Panamanians, who may not believe all of the folktales, consider All Souls' Day to be an important time for reverence and reflection.

BIRTH AND DEATH Folk believers and Roman Catholics alike place great importance on birth and death, and they commemorate these events with religious liturgies. Baptism is the most significant religious ceremony as it symbolizes the infant's entry into society and the church. Rural Panamanians believe so strongly in the importance of baptism that entire families often travel for miles to a parish center. A child's First Communion is also an important event. Children attend classes to prepare them for their First Communion and subsequent involvement in the church.

Death also is an important event that Panamanians mark with a religious ceremony. Even if a person has not been a devout Catholic, a priest will often administer last rites anyway. This tradition is important to those who believe that they will appear before the devil and God on All Souls' Day because their last contact on Earth was with a religious figure.

The deceased's family has the body embalmed and displayed for mourners to view. After a few days of visits, the family holds services in the church or a selected place of worship. The mourners then form a procession and follow the pallbearers to the grave site.

INTERNET LINKS

www.panama-guide.com/article.php/20060427223159815
This site has photos of the Golden Altar of the Church of San Jose in Casco Viejo, Panama City.

www.pewforum.org/2014/11/13/religion-in-latin-america
This article by the Pew Research Center is about the decline of Catholicism in Latin America, but includes statistics about Panama.

www.state.gov/documents/organization/171789.pdf
The US State Department offers information about religions in Panama.

LANGUAGES

A sign on the border with Colombia announces, "Welcome to Panama."

ALMOST EVERYONE IN PANAMA speaks Spanish, the country's official language. Many also speak another language, either their indigenous or native language or English. Around 14 percent of the population cites English as their native tongue, while Spanish is used in government, trade, and education. Many Panamanians—particularly the wealthy— are fluent in English because of the former US presence in the Canal Zone. Some use English only in business settings. The Afro-Caribbeans, who originally came to Panama from the West Indies, have retained their English tongue as well. Apart from Spanish and English, Panamanians also speak nine Amerindian, or indigenous, languages.

Panama is a Latin American country, and Panamanians refer to their region as Latinoamérica. They call all of the Spanish- speaking countries of the Americas Hispanoamérica and the people hispanoamericanos.

CARIBBEAN SPANISH

Although Spanish is the official language of Panama, it's not quite the same Spanish as is spoken in Spain. There is no "one-size-fits-all"

español, or Spanish language, in the world. The type spoken in Panama is usually classified by linguists as Caribbean Spanish, as opposed to *castellano*, or Castilian, the Spanish of Spain. However, many Latin Americans use the term *castellano* to describe their language.

Caribbean Spanish is the form of the language spoken in Cuba, Puerto Rico, and the Dominican Republic, as well as in Panama, Venezuela, and along the Caribbean coast of Colombia. Curiously, there is another dialect called Central American Spanish, but this is not descriptive of Panamanian speech, even though Panama is located in Central America. Rather, the Central American form is spoken in Costa Rica, El Salvador, Guatemala, Honduras, and Nicaragua.

Guna children learn Spanish at a bilingual school for indigenous students in Ustupo, a town in Guna Yala province.

LANGUAGES OF THE INDIGENOUS PEOPLE

The Native groups have their own dialects and their Native languages are protected by Panama's constitution, which requires the government to provide bilingual literacy programs in indigenous communities. The Guna speak both Spanish and their native tongue, Guna. The Gunas tend to speak quickly and accent the last syllable of a word. The Ngöbe-Buglé people speak a language called Morere, or "language of the plains." Over 50 percent of the Ngöbe-Buglés speak Morere and Spanish, while the remaining speak only Spanish. Emberá is the native tongue of the Emberá people. Other Panamanians, such as the East Indians and Chinese, tend to speak their own country's native tongues. For the most part, however, Panamanians speak either Spanish or both Spanish and English.

THE SPANISH LANGUAGE

The Spanish alphabet has twenty-eight letters: a, b, c, ch, d, e, f, g, h i, j, l, ll, m, n, ñ, o, p, q, r, rr, s, t, u, v, x, y, *and* z. *The Spanish alphabet does not contain the English letters* k *or* w. *Some words of foreign origin, such as* kilo *and* kilómetro, *use the letter* k. *Otherwise, the Spanish letter* c *sounds like the English* k *unless* e *or* i *follows it (then it sounds like the English* s*).*

Like the English alphabet, the Spanish one has five vowels that the letters a, e, i, o, *and* u *represent. Each vowel has one basic sound:*

a	*is pronounced like the* a *in "father"*
e	*is pronounced like the* ai *in "train"*
i	*is pronounced like the* ee *in "teeth"*
o	*is pronounced like the* o *in "slow"*
u	*is pronounced like the* u *in "dude"*

Many of the consonants of the Spanish language are similar to their English counterparts. Some notable differences are:

b *and* v *are interchangeable. If a word begins with either a* b *or a* v, *it sounds like the* b *in "boy." If either letter falls in the middle or the end of a sentence, it is pronounced like the* v *in "devil."*

d *sounds like its English counterpart unless it is between two vowels. Then, it sounds like the* th *in "thank."*

g *sounds like the* g *in "girl." If an* e *or* i *follows a* g, *however, then it sounds like* h *in "hello."*

h *is silent in Spanish.*

j *sounds like the English* h *as in "house."*

ll, *which is a single letter in the Spanish language, is pronounced as an English* y, *as in "yard."*

ñ *sounds like the* ny *in "canyon."*

r, *in Spanish, is a slightly rolled, but very quickly spoken letter.*

rr *is the* r *sound strongly trilled.*

z *resembles the English* s *in song.*

A Spanish-language newspaper headlines "National Unity" over a photo of the new president, Juan Carlos Varela, in 2014.

MEDIA AND COMMUNICATIONS

Panama has five major daily newspapers, multiple privately owned TV networks and a government-owned educational TV station, as well as multi-channel cable and satellite TV service. There are more than one hundred commercial radio stations, all but one privately owned. In 2014, some 48.4 percent of the Panamanian population used the internet.

The Panamanian press provides wide-ranging information to Panamanians, including international and domestic news, political commentaries, editorials, and special features. The Panamanian constitution protects the freedom of speech and of the press. Media laws penalizing journalists for showing disrespect to certain government officials were abolished in 2005, when President Guillermo Endara reinstated freedom of the press after the Noriega regime had forced many media personnel to leave Panama. Nevertheless, in 2015, Freedom House, an organization that rates press freedom worldwide, gave Panama a score of only 49 (or "Partly

Free") out of 100, with 0 being the best and 100 being the worst possible score. The group attributes this less than stellar score to "laws that allow for the prosecution of journalists for vaguely defined offenses related to the exposure of private information, and prescribe severe penalties for leaking government information to the press." The report admits, however that the atmosphere for journalists is much safer in Panama than in many neighboring Central American nations.

GREETINGS

Panamanians are polite. They pay attention to greetings and formalities in their everyday life. For instance, a business person always makes small talk with a colleague or client before discussing business. Panamanians are offended if anyone initiates a business conversation before they have spent enough time learning about the other party on a personal level. Panamanians of either sex may greet each other by shaking hands. Female friends typically kiss each other on one cheek when greeting and departing. Men and women sometimes kiss each other on the cheek, but two men always shake hands. The tradition of kissing on one cheek differs from the South American tradition of kissing another person on both cheeks. Usually the kiss is an "air-kiss," and the people do not actually let their lips touch the other's cheek.

Panamanians are very gracious and polite. They frequently say "please" or "*por favor*," "thank you" or "*gracias*," and "you're welcome" or "*de nada*." Before joining a group of people who are eating or conversing, a newcomer will ask permission to join the group by saying "*con permiso*" (kohn pair-MEE-soh). The group responds by saying "*andele*," (AHN-day-lay) meaning "go ahead."

CONVERSATION

The discussion of personal possessions is one of the major taboos in Panamanian conversation. Unlike other nationalities, the people of Panama are not interested in discussing status and money matters with one another. Another topic that Panamanians avoid, especially with American citizens,

Two athletes shake hands at a wheelchair basketball championship game.

is the building of the canal and the US intervention. Panamanians generally do not like to discuss local politics and race in social settings. Their favorite conversational topics include family, common friends, hobbies, interests, and sports, such as basketball and baseball.

NONVERBAL COMMUNICATION

Nonverbal behavior and gestures are an important part of Panamanian communication. While many of the gestures are similar to those in the United States, some are noteworthy.

Shaking hands upon meeting someone shows good manners; this greeting can be done in two ways—either the standard handshake, or a grip similar to an arm wrestling position. When Panamanians want another person to approach them, they will raise one of their hands with the palm facing the other person. This gesture resembles the North American wave.

PANAMANIAN NAMES

Panamanians have two surnames, or family names, after their first name. The first is the father's surname, and the second is the mother's surname. Thus, if a child is named Ana María and her mother's family name is Chavez and her father's family name is Gonzalez, her name will be Ana María Gonzalez Chavez. In formal situations, Panamanians will use the second surname. Thus, Ana María would go by Ana María Chavez on formal occasions.

When a couple marries, the woman adds her husband's first surname, that of his father, to her own first surname. A woman keeps her own first surname to honor her family and pass the name along to her children. The word *de*, meaning "of," precedes her husband's surname. If Ana María marries a man named Juan Federico Nuñez Alvarez, her new name will be either Ana María de Nuñez or Ana María Gonzalez de Nuñez. Her husband, Juan, will retain his name, and their children will use Nuñez as the first surname and Gonzalez as the second surname.

FORMS OF ADDRESS

Panamanians address others based on the person's social status and familiarity. While the English language has one word for the second person— "you"—Spanish has two words: the familiar *tu* or the formal *usted*. When Panamanians meet a person who is the same age or older, they refer to the person as *usted*. As they become friends, they call each other *tu*. Panamanians usually use *tu* to address a younger person that they are meeting for the first time, unless the younger person is prestigious. Persons from a lower class will almost always call a person of higher status *usted*.

INTERNET LINKS

freedomhouse.org/report/freedom-press/2015/panama
This is the 2015 report on freedom of the press in Panama.

www.omniglot.com/language/articles/latin_american_spanish.htm
Omniglot gives an overview of the categories of Spanish found in Latin America.

www.veintemundos.com/en/spanish/panama/
This language learning site offers an overview of Panamanian Spanish and other languages, including a few common phrases.

ARTS

The renovated Las Clementinas, a hotel in the Casco Viejo section of Panama City, exhibits tropical architectural flair.

10

A COUNTRY'S ART AND LITERATURE reflect its political and cultural identities. Because Spain, and then Colombia, controlled Panama before its independence in the early twentieth century, Panamanian arts from these times often exhibit influences from these two countries. When the Spanish colonists arrived in Panama, they not only killed thousands of native people, but also destroyed the indigenous art. The colonists believed European culture was superior and therefore mimicked Spanish art and architecture when building new towns in Panama.

Around the seventeenth century, Panamanians began to reject the Spanish influence and develop a culture of their own. Many great artists, authors, and poets emerged during that period. These artists imitated contemporary art from European countries other than Spain. African art also influenced Panamanian art during this period because of the large number of enslaved Africans who had been brought into the country.

When Panama finally became independent in the early twentieth century, the country no longer squelched primitive artistic expressions.

Ricardo Miró (1883-1940) is considered Panama's greatest poet, and one of his poems, "Patria," ("Homeland") arouses national unity and pride in Panamanians of all ages today. In honor of Miró's contribution to Panamanian literature, a prestigious award, the Premio Ricardo Miró, is given every year to outstanding authors.

One of the colorful painted buses of Panama City is an example of the iconic folk art tradition of the chivas.

Panamanians became proud of their indigenous art, as well as the success that indigenous people achieved in literature, ballet, and sculpture. Artists and authors incorporated indigenous art into their works.

FOLK CULTURE

Panama has an extensive folk culture that reflects Spanish, African, North American, and West Indian influences. Some of its folk culture and art are displayed in galleries and museums.

Besides museums, city buses also display art exhibits. The Panamanians purchase yellow school buses from the United States and turn them into wonderfully decorated modes of transportation called *chivas* (CHEE-vahs). The art of painting buses began after World War II, and these vehicles have become an integral part of the country's transportation system. They are also widely featured in Panamanian literature. The artists begin to decorate the buses by painting over the original yellow coating. They then paint long images, such as a mermaid, a panoramic scene, or a dragon on the side. The rear emergency door forms the crux of the artwork, and the artist sometimes devotes this area to religious illustrations.

Native groups produce traditional crafts like woodcarvings, weavings, ceramics, and masks. In addition to making molas, which are world-renowned appliquéd and embroidered fabrics, the Guna people of the San Blas Islands also create sculptures, clay pottery, and baskets. The Ngöbe-Buglé people sell exquisite jewelry crafted from bones, shells, or glass. Their specialty is the *chaquira* (chah-KEE-rah), which is a multicolored beaded necklace. The Wounaan and Emberá people of the Darién rain forest weave gorgeous patterned baskets from the fibers of the nahuala plant and chunga palm.

TEXTILE ART OF THE GUNA

In the Guna language, mola *literally means "clothing," but the word also refers to a distinctive textile art that Guna women have been making for centuries. Intricately appliquéd and embroidered fabrics are incorporated into clothing, such as a panel of a blouse. Today, the colorful fabrics are renowned for their exquisite detail, fine stitching, and bright colors. Mola production has become a major industry and source of income.*

The Gunas believe that all things have a spirit, so the mola maker takes great pride in creating a spirit for her mola. She often integrates many elements, such as animals, insects, birds, plants, religious scenes, and legends, into her design. Sometimes, her design might be geometrical. Common themes for a mola design include world events, religious scenery, and nature. Some Guna designs are passed down from one generation to the next.

The Guna expect women to be good mola makers. Young girls begin creating molitas, *or "little molas," by the time they are six or seven. In this way, the women hand down their intricate sewing skills from one generation to the next. If a girl doesn't become an adept mola maker, the medicine man will hold a ceremony and burn certain herbs to help her improve.*

The average mola measures 16 by 24 inches (41 by 61 cm). Despite its relatively small size, several months are required to secure the layers of the panel with tiny stitches. The process of making a mola is quite elaborate. First, the maker stacks and stitches two to seven layers of colored fabric together before drawing or visualizing the design on the top piece. Then, she cuts out various designs to reveal the colored layers underneath. Finally, she adds the final touches using embroidery or appliqué. The end result is a beautiful and colorful mola that she may keep or sell.

Molas have become highly valued folk art, and many museums have collections of them. A number of internet sites sell molas online.

THE ORAL TRADITION OF STORYTELLING

Panamanian children look forward to the Feast of All Souls' Day, which is the equivalent of Halloween in the United States. Traditionally, on All Souls' Day a group of children gather around an adult who tells superstitious tales and frightening stories. Usually the adult will claim to have witnessed whatever event is described in the story.

The storyteller usually begins the story by asking the children if they have taken care of their familiars, which are invisible beings that surround people. If so, the familiars will remain good. However, if the children neglect their familiars, these invisible beings may turn to evil.

After the first question, the storyteller draws the children in by altering the tone of voice, pausing at important moments, and using hand gestures. The children often become so enthralled by the story that they huddle around the storyteller and hang on every word. Usually, their eyes are transfixed on the storyteller, not only because they are intrigued by the story, but also because they fear that evil spirits might be lurking behind their backs.

The stories are suspenseful, frightening, and often so gruesome that the youngest listeners will cover their ears. Storytelling is an important oral tradition for Panamanians, and children will retell the stories that they heard to their own children. Storytelling is often a bonding experience for both young and old, as they spend quality time together without distractions from the television or radio.

MUSIC AND DANCE

Song and dance form a significant part of Panama's culture. Music in Panama is a pulsating fusion of many styles, including salsa, Cuban son, Colombian cumbia, Argentine tango, and Caribbean ska, reggae, and soca. Drums, castanets, bells, and small, five-stringed guitars called *mejoranas* (may-hoh-RAH-nas) produce the sound. The mejorana is both the instrument and the type of music itself. Both originated in Spain in the eighteenth century.

Panama's national dance is the *tamborito* (tam-boh-REE-toh), which differs from region to region. The tamborito, meaning "little drum," originated in Spain in the seventeenth century, but the Panamanian version integrates African rhythms. The dancers perform the tamborito to the rhythm of clapping hands and pounding drumbeats.

Popular throughout Latin America, the *cumbia* (KOOM-byah), is a music genre and folk dance that originated in Colombia/Panama during the Spanish colonial era. It incorporates elements of European, African, and indigenous dance and music. It can be performed as a group circle dance, or as a partner dance for couples. In a circle, some as large as forty people, the men dance in the center and the women on the outside. The dancers take tiny steps and rotate to the sound of drums and maracas, or pebble-filled gourds.

Folk dancers perform at a restaurant in Panama City.

Folk dancers usually wear elaborate costumes for their performances, sometimes wearing traditional African apparel to showcase the strong African influence. A lot of gold and pearl jewelry, featuring designs from the Native groups, is also worn.

ARCHITECTURE AND MUSEUMS

Panama has a variety of architectural styles ranging from Spanish colonial buildings to modern glass skyscrapers. Rural houses are built to minimize heat and maximize ventilation. Panama City has the widest assortment of architecture, which gives the city its unique and eclectic look.

Buildings constructed over three hundred years ago still stand in the old section, Casco Viejo. The city's older areas resemble Spanish colonial towns, with stucco, wrought-iron work, abundant balconies, and cobblestone streets. The newer portions of Panama City feature sleek boulevards, magnificent glass and concrete high-rises, and large apartment buildings.

The Presidential Palace, the *Palacio de las Garzas* ("Palace of the Herons") is one of the most striking buildings in Panama City. Built in 1673, its Moorish balconies are decked in mother-of-pearl, and the famous Panamanian artist

Panama's favorite and most famous musician, bar none, is the "King of Salsa," Rubén Blades (b. 1948). In fact, he may well be Panama's favorite overall celebrity, because he is also a singer, songwriter, actor, activist, and politician. In 1994, he ran unsuccessfully for president of Panama; however, in 2014, he suggested that he might run again in the 2019 elections. From 2004 to 2009, he served as Panama's tourism minister under President Martin Torrijos.

First and foremost, however, Blades is known and loved for his music, which he calls "thinking persons' dance music." Salsa, which originated in Latin America, is an upbeat musical form that blends rock, jazz, and rhythm and blues with Cuban rhythms.

Blades grew up in a poor neighborhood in Panama City. He began his singing career as the frontman for a local band and also sang jingles for Panamanian beer commercials. When Manuel Noriega accused Blades's father of being a CIA agent, the family fled to Miami, Florida.

Blades joined his family in Florida after completing his law degree at the University of Panama. He then moved to New York City to become a professional musician and

eventually earned international fame as a salsa singer in the mid-1970s. After achieving success in the music world, he earned a master's degree in international law at Harvard University in 1985, and went on to make movies in Hollywood. Throughout his many careers, Rubén Blades remained true to his homeland by writing songs about the common people's struggles with poverty.

Among his many awards and accomplishments, Blades has won eight Grammy Awards, including Best Latin Pop Album for his 2014 album, Tango, *and five Latin Grammy Awards; released more than fifty albums; appeared in a number of TV shows, including AMC's* Fear the Walking Dead *(2015); and acted in forty-two feature films, including* Hands of Stone *(2016).*

Roberto Lewis painted the murals. Beautiful gardens and fountains adorn the the palace grounds.

Panama City's culture is as varied as its architecture. Besides gambling casinos and racetracks, Panama City is also home to several wonderful museums. The Reina Torres de Araúz Anthropological Museum displays relics from the Spanish occupation, vestiges of pre-Columbian cultures, and archaeological artifacts from hundreds of indigenous groups.

The Museum of the Panamanian in downtown Panama City is another impressive place. It traces the country's history from precolonial times to the building of the Panama Canal and beyond. It also documents the evolution of human life on the isthmus, from the earliest native settlements to the present ethnically diverse population.

INTERNET LINKS

www.justlanded.com/english/Panama/Panama-Guide/Culture/ Traditional-dances-of-Panama
This site gives a quick overview of three popular dances.

www.npr.org/artists/15283727/ruben-blades
This NPR page lists audio links to ten of its radio programs about or mentioning Rubén Blades.

www.panamasimple.com/palace-of-the-herons
The presidential Palace of the Herons is featured on this page.

www.panart.com
This site features a variety of indigenous art, including molas and baskets, showing portraits of the artisans as well.

sanblas-islands.com/kuna-indians/art
This site includes information about and images of the mola fabric art of the Guna.

LEISURE

A man snorkels in the Caribbean Sea off the Panama coast.

11

PANAMANIANS ENJOY A WIDE VARIETY
of pastimes, from simple picnics
with family and friends to visiting art
museums to playing or watching sports.
Panama's range of topography enables
its citizens to enjoy all sorts of outdoor
activities, on land and at sea.

The mountains of Panama provide a haven for fitness enthusiasts. Panama's highest mountain, the Volcán Barú, attracts many hikers and rock climbers. The Volcán Barú is a long-dormant volcano, so many guides offer exploration treks through the crater. There are several thermal springs and cool lagoons in the mountains. The numerous rivers and streams are ideal for white-water rafting and fishing. Many people enjoy hunting and bird-watching in the mountains.

As the narrowest stretch of land between the Atlantic and Pacific Oceans, Panama offers a wealth of water activities. People can even swim in the Atlantic in the morning, and dive in the Pacific in the afternoon! The Atlantic Ocean offers the most scenic scuba diving spots, thanks to the abundant coral growing in its warmer waters. Near Portobelo, divers may explore several wrecked ships that are submerged underwater. The San Blas, Contadora, and Taboga Islands are blessed with superb beaches. Panamanians enjoy sailing and surfing in all the waters around the country.

Inland, Gatún Lake offers water activities from sailing to fishing. The lake, which was built to accommodate the Panama Canal and is the second largest artificial lake in the world, is an excellent site for freshwater bass fishing.

"It might be because of my childhood, how hard it was. Every time I jump into the ring, I see a whole picture of how it was."
—Panamanian boxing hero Roberto Durán, commenting in 1980 on the fierce rage that fueled his fighting

Mariano Rivera wears a minor league team shirt during a visit to one of its games.

Panama's name means "abundance of fish," and the sheer number of species attracts many fishing enthusiasts. Deep-sea sports fishers know the waters off Panama's Pacific coast as "the black marlin capital of the world." Other popular catches include the striped marlin, dolphin, roosterfish, wahoo, and rainbow runners.

NATIONAL SPECTATOR SPORTS

The most popular spectator sports in Panama are baseball, basketball, soccer, boxing, horse racing, cockfighting, and dog racing. Panamanians are passionate spectators and players of their national sport, baseball. Like Americans, Panamanians also enjoy watching the World Series and they support fellow citizens who have successful careers abroad. A number of Panamanians have played in the North American major leagues, including Hall of Famer Rod Carew and former New York Yankees pitcher Mariano Rivera (b. 1969). Panamanians also enjoy soccer; but unlike their neighbor, Colombia, they do not consider soccer to be the national sport.

Panama has been successful in the international sports arena. The country has produced several champion boxers. Its weight lifters, track and field athletes, basketball players, and swimmers have also achieved success at the Pan-American Games. Panama usually sends a small contingent of athletes to the Olympic Summer Games; it has never participated in the Winter Olympics.

URBAN ENTERTAINMENT

Urban Panamanians enjoy city-based activities. They have many types of leisure activities to choose from, including shopping, theater, music, nightclubs, and casinos.

ROBERTO DURÁN'S HANDS OF STONE

Panama's all-time sports hero is Roberto Durán (b. 1951). This four-time world champion boxer was born in El Chorrillo and grew up poor on the Panamanian side of the Canal Zone. Durán began his boxing career as an amateur, and the boxing federation chose him to represent Panama in the Pan-American Games when he was sixteen years old. But Durán would not obey certain etiquette rules and was kicked out. This incident provided the first glimpse into the volatile and aggressive personality of a man who would one day be a hero to millions.

Durán turned professional in 1968. He won his first world championship title just four years later. His powerful punches earned him the nickname "Manos de Piedra" ("Hands of Stone").

Durán won the World Boxing Association welterweight title in 1980, when he defeated Sugar Ray Leonard. He was the first to defeat Leonard in the professional boxing ring, and Panama erupted in wild celebration. Five months after the first fight, the boxers met again. This time Durán surprised everyone by refusing to continue in the eighth round, muttering "no más" ("no more"). Three years later, Durán came back and earned another world championship title. With this historic victory, Durán became the first boxer to win titles in both the lightweight and junior middleweight divisions.

When he was thirty-seven years old, he won his fourth title by beating middleweight champion Iran Barkley of the United States. Once again, Panamanians celebrated.

Despite his often explosive personality, many Panamanians idolize Durán. After being injured in a car accident, he retired in January 2002 at the age of fifty-two. He was elected to the World Boxing Hall of Fame and the International Boxing Hall of Fame in 2006 and 2007. Hands of Stone, *a movie about Durán's life—starring Édgar Ramírez as the boxer; Robert De Niro as his trainer, the legendary Ray Arcel; and pop star Usher as Sugar Ray Leonard—premiered at the Cannes Film Festival in May 2016.*

SHOPPING Panama City has been called the "Hong Kong of Latin America" because prices are low, while the quantity and quality of goods are high. The main shopping area is a street called Vía España. Another popular shopping spot is Avenida Central, where Panamanians can find many electronic and camera stores. Popular shopping items include cameras, electronic goods, perfumes, watches, china, jewelry, mola fabric, leather goods, weavings, and baskets. One difference between shopping in the United States and shopping in Panama is that bargaining with the seller for a lower price is widely accepted in Panama.

Due to the fact that Panama City is a major tourist destination, many hotels feature shopping centers. Panamanians, however, tend to shy away from these areas to avoid the tourists. Like Spain, the shops in Panama close for lunch and a siesta, or nap, every afternoon. Most shops are open from 8 a.m. until noon, then reopen at 2 p.m., before closing at 6 or 7 in the evening.

THEATER AND MUSIC Many Panamanians enjoy attending theater and musical events. For stage shows, Panamanians go to the National Theater in Panama City's colonial district. During February and March, the Folklore Ballet performs there. The dancers perform native folk dances in traditional costume. Panama also has movie theaters that show Panamanian and US movies. Although many Panamanians are bilingual, English movies often have Spanish subtitles.

Music is an integral part of Panamanian life. Panamanians enjoy listening to salsa music and other types of popular music. Panama City is home to the National Symphony, and the city also hosts many outdoor concerts.

NIGHTLIFE Restaurants, bars, and casinos are widely found throughout Panama. The dance clubs and nightclubs frequently stay open all night so that night owls can party until dawn.

Panama's government operates its casinos in Panama City. Like Las Vegas, the casinos attract more tourists than locals. Most of the city's casinos are located in hotels or at the airport. The Panamanian government does not tax people on the money that they win from gambling.

RURAL ENTERTAINMENT

Rural Panamanians play sports and make handicrafts during their leisure time. Local towns often have baseball and soccer leagues for children and adults. Because many rural towns are located in beautiful mountainous regions, local residents often hike and bike through the countryside.

The Native groups that reside in rural Panama participate in gender-based leisure activities. The men hunt and fish, while the women make pottery, arts, crafts, and molas. Many of these activities overlap with the groups' occupations.

WEEKEND RETREATS

City dwellers often seek tranquility in the countryside and at the beaches. Panamanians have sixteen annual holidays when businesses, banks, and

Locals and tourists enjoy diving at Los Cangilones de Gualaca, a "mini canyon" in the Chiriqui province.

COCKFIGHTING: POPULAR SPORT OR ANIMAL ABUSE?

Many Panamanians enjoy watching and betting on cockfighting. In this activity, popular throughout Latin America, trained gamecocks fight each other with their beaks and legs. The animals usually have razor-sharp spurs attached to their legs, which they use to try to injure one another. Cockfighting involves either pitting two roosters against each other or several birds fighting in a group. The fight comes to an end when one or more of the gamecocks dies or refuses to fight anymore.

Cockfighting is big business and the bird owners, trainers, and spectators take it very seriously. A great deal of money changes hands as large bets are placed, won, or lost, on the animal fights. The blood sport is a legacy, along with bullfighting, that the Spanish brought to the Americas centuries ago.

Despite the tremendous popularity of cockfighting, some Panamanians are calling for it to be banned, as it is in Costa Rica. Many people consider the entertainment to be cruel animal abuse.

government offices are closed. Some people often take a few extra days off before or after a holiday to spend long weekends in the countryside.

Some favorite vacation spots include the Taboga and Contadora Islands, the San Blas Islands, and the beaches along the Caribbean Sea and the Pacific Ocean. Taboga is located off the shore of Panama City. Tourists and locals alike flock to its beautiful beaches for sunbathing and water activities. Contadora is also located in the Gulf of Panama and serves as a relaxing holiday spot, as well as an international summit center. In the 1980s, several Latin American leaders met there to discuss common problems in their countries, and they became known as the Contadora Group.

The beaches along the Pacific and Atlantic coasts are popular retreats. Panama is building many new deluxe hotels and casinos to attract both foreign and domestic vacationers to these areas.

FITNESS

Like people in many Western countries, Panamanians have become increasingly concerned about their health. In response to the fitness craze, many cities have built more recreational facilities. Wealthy Panamanians often play tennis and golf in their own country, or go skiing in neighboring South American countries. Some middle-class Panamanians also play golf and tennis, or venture abroad for skiing. Panamanians' favorite ski destinations are Portillo, Chile, and Bariloche, Argentina. Because the South American countries are located below the equator, the winter ski season runs from July to September.

INTERNET LINKS

espn.go.com/mlb/worldclassic2006/news/story?id=2291367
"Welcome to Panama" offers some interesting Panamanian baseball facts and information.

www.huffingtonpost.com/2014/05/05/daily-life-panama_n_5268426.html
This photo essay peeks at daily life in Panama.

www.nytimes.com/packages/html/sports/year_in_sports/11.25.html
"The Champ Throws in the Towel" by Red Smith vividly relates the famous incident of Roberto Durán's "no más" loss to Sugar Ray Leonard in 1980.

FESTIVALS

In Los Santos, a festive parade commemorates the Call of Independence on November 10.

12

I N PANAMA, A HOLIDAY OR CELEBRATION is called a fiesta. Some are festive parties, as the word fiesta suggests in English, while others are serious events that honor religious figures. Fiestas i Panama generally fall into two categories, religious holidays linked to the Roman Catholic Church calendar, and national observances. November is particularly packed with national celebrations, with three different independence holidays as well as Colón Day and Flag Day. Together they are called the Fiestas Patrias. Major religious celebrations include the Easter and Christmas holidays, while smaller fiestas honor various saints on their respective feast days throughout the year.

The Native peoples of Panama have their own festivals that incorporate both religious and secular beliefs. These festivals are often lively events featuring much music and dance, and occasionally even contests and fighting.

In addition, certain events in a Panamanian's life, such as birth, First Communion, marriage, and death, are each celebrated with a fiesta.

On November 10, 1821, a young woman named Rufina Alfaro led a march for independence in the town of Los Santos. Shouting "Viva La Libertad," ("Long Live Liberty") she inspired the townspeople to overthrow their Spanish leaders. Today November 10 is celebrated throughout Panama as First Call of Independence Day. However, no one is certain whether Alfaro actually existed or if she is merely a legendary figure.

CALENDAR OF FIESTAS IN PANAMA

January 1	New Year's Day	national holiday
January 9	Martyrs' Day (National Day of Mourning)	For the lives lost in the January 9, 1964 riots over sovereignty of the Panama Canal Zone / national holiday
February (dates vary)	Carnival	Four-day revelry before the start of the austere Lenten season leading to Holy Week. The final day, Shrove Tuesday, or Mardi Gras, is a national holiday.
March/April (dates vary)	Holy Week, Good Friday, Easter	The crucifixion and resurrection of Christ
May 1	May Day/Labor Day	workers /national holiday
August 15	Founding of Panama City	Local holiday
November 3	Independence Day	Independence from Colombia / national holiday
November 4	Flag Day	Local holidays
November 5	Colón Day (Columbus Day)	The arrival of Christopher Columbus, or Cristóbal Colón, in the Americas / national holiday
November 10	First Call of Independence Day (Shout in Villa de los Santos Day)	The uprising led by Rufina Alfaro/ national holiday
November 28	Independence from Spain Day	National holiday
December 8	Mother's Day	Feast of the Immaculate Conception / national holiday
December 24	Christmas Eve	bank holiday
December 25	Christmas Day	The birth of Jesus / national holiday
December 31	New Year's Eve	bank holiday

CARNIVAL

Carnival is the grandest fiesta in the Panamanian calendar. This rollicking celebration takes place for four days before Ash Wednesday, the start of the Lenten season. Lent is the solemn religious observance of the forty days leading to Easter. Roman Catholics often observe some form of penitence or devotion during this time, such as giving up meat, or a favorite food or activity. Therefore, in anticipation of the austerity to come, Carnival is a time to drink, eat, and party.

All the Central and South American countries celebrate Carnival. The jubilee began when Spanish and West African traditions merged in the New World. The West African slaves took advantage of the four-day Spanish holiday to revel in their brief freedom. They turned this time into an elaborate celebration with costumes, traditional music, and dance. Today Carnival is one of the biggest festivals in the world.

In Panama, Carnival resembles Mardi Gras in New Orleans. Celebrations consist of *comparsas* (cohm-PAHR-sahs), or groups of people dancing, partying, and playing instruments in the streets. Bands play salsa, reggae,

The queen of Carnival in Penonomé wears a typically elaborate costume.

THE FESTIVAL OF THE BLACK CHRIST OF PORTOBELO

According to Panamanian legend, a wood carving of the Black Christ (Cristo Negro, also known as El Nazareno) from a shipwrecked Spanish galleon washed up onto the shores of Portobelo. The fishermen believed that the statue ended a devastating cholera outbreak in the town. As a token of gratitude, they promised to hold an annual festival in its honor. Portobelo's inhabitants and thousands of pilgrims from all over Panama continue to honor the Black Christ during the Festival of the Black Christ on October 21 every year.

On that day, hundreds of people carry the statue of the Black Christ on a platform. These people spend four hours walking through town. For every three steps that they take forward, they must take two steps back. Thousands of people come to venerate the statue each year, particularly on this date, and many miracles have been ascribed to it. Most of the pilgrims and worshippers wear purple robes similar to the one on the Black Christ. The parade ends at the stroke of midnight at the home of the Black Christ statue—the Church of San Felipe, built in 1814—when the statue is finally returned for another year to its place beside the golden altar inside.

and Panamanian folkloric music, and each day features a parade, with the biggest one taking place on the final day, Shrove Tuesday, or Mardi Gras.

Some of the comparsas wear elaborate and colorful costumes, which require months of preparation. A favorite mesn's costume includes a multi-colored papier-mâché mask, a black vest over a white shirt, black pants with ribbons tied criss-cross around the calf, an orange or red sash draped across the torso, and a colorful, full skirt made of strips of fabric resembling a man's tie. Men who prefer a simpler costume would put on guayabera shirts, comfortable black pants, sandals, and a straw hat. The women usually wear the *pollera de gala* or "deluxe" *pollera*—a traditional, embroidered full skirt—for Carnival, complete with headpieces and jewelry made of gold and pearls.

Part of Carnival tradition is the *mojaderas*, which involves getting drenched in water. Tanker trucks shower the crowds while revelers spray one another with water pistols and hoses. Some also carry bags of confetti to toss at passersby. Many tourists head to Panama City for the festivities, but locals consider Las Tablas, the capital of Los Santos, to be the best location. Featuring dramatic costumes, inventive floats, spectacular fireworks, and festive music, this city is renowned for hosting the noisiest and liveliest Carnival celebration in Panama.

INDEPENDENCE DAYS

Panama has two different independence days. On November 3, the country celebrates its independence from Colombia, while it celebrates its independence from Spain on November 28. Parades, fiestas, and fireworks feature prominently on these two days, as well as on the other patriotic commerations of the *Feistas Patrias*, Flag Day, November 4, and First Call of Independence Day on November 10. Government offices, businesses, and shops close on these days so that employees may join in the festivities. Peole gather at Independence Square in Panama City for rallies and speeches, and the streets are decorated with flags and draped in the national colors.

INTERNET LINKS

www.aswesawit.com/panama-carnival
This travel site features a firsthand look at Carnival events in Panama, with many photos.

www.coloncity.com/blackchrist.html
This page relates the story of the Black Christ statue at the church in Portobelo.

playacommunity.com/news-mainmenu-149/community-news-mainmenu-214/4627-panamanians-christmas-and-new-year-traditions
Christmas and New Year's traditions in Panama are explained on this Panama news site.

www.vacationtopanama.com/travel-guide/top-5-cultural-events
This travel site lists the "Top 5 Cultural Events in Panama."

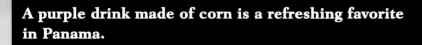

FOOD

A purple drink made of corn is a refreshing favorite in Panama.

13

FOOD IS A NECESSITY, BUT CUISINE— the way food is prepared in any given region—is cultural. Panama's cuisine reflects the food cultures of the African, Spanish, and native peoples who have lived in this place over time. Unlike the cooking of some of its Latin American and Caribbean spicier neighbors, Panama's cuisine tends to be mildly flavored.

Panama's chief agricultural products are rice, corn, beans, and coffee. These locally grown products are staples in the diet. Panamanians have *arroz* (ah-ROHS), or rice, with most of their meals, especially for lunch. They either eat the rice plain, or add meat and vegetables to it. Panamanians often consume both potatoes and rice in the same meal.

Panamanians also eat corn in a variety of ways. Tortillas are the most popular corn-based product, and are made by grinding the corn into flour before mixing it with water. The paste is then formed into thick pancakes called tortillas. The Panamanian tortilla is thick and fried, unlike the thinner Mexican version. Like many other Latin Americans, Panamanians top their tortillas with cheese, meats, and vegetables to make a variety of dishes. Most Panamanian meals include corn tortillas or rice with meat and vegetables, or fruit.

Yucca, the starchy tuber of the cassava plant, is a commonly served vegetable. Cilantro (also called coriander leaf) is often added to soup and sauces for flavor. Other common vegetables are onions, peppers,

Panamanians enjoy a variety of freshly squeezed fruit juices and drinks, called *chichas*. They are made from the many tropical fruits in that region, including papayas, bananas, passionfruits, watermelons, and pineapples. A *batido* is a milk-based drink made with a fruit puree, and is something like a fruit smoothie. A popular one in Panama is made with pineapple, white rice, milk, and sugar blended with a little cinnamon.

A young fisherman holds a cleaned snapper in Chiriqui Province in western Panama.

corn, and tomatoes. There are many varieties of fruit in Panama, including pineapples, coconuts, papayas, avocados, watermelons, and citrus fruits.

True to its name, Panama enjoys an abundance of fish and seafood. The country's shrimp and lobster are superb, as are the marlin, sea bass, and snapper. The oceans and freshwater lakes provide a ready supply of fish for consumption. Chicken and beef are also popular types of meat.

KITCHENS

Many affluent Panamanians employ live-in maids to help them with domestic matters, such as cooking and cleaning. The maid, or the domestic helper, prepares the meal and serves it to the family in the formal dining room.

The kitchens in rural Panama are simple and often include little more than a stove and a countertop. Over the past few decades, the government has provided running water to many rural communities. Some people, however, must still walk to the community well to obtain clean water. The Ngöbe-Buglé people prepare their meals in a building that is separate from their house. Sometimes more than one family will share the cooking facility in a Ngöbe-Buglé community.

EATING OUT

Panamanians love to eat out, and there is a plethora of restaurants in the cities. A *restaurante* (res-tow-RAN-tay) is similar to a restaurant in the United States, a *panadería* (pan-ah-day-REE-ah) sells take-out bread and rolls, a *pastelería* (pas-tell-ay-REE-ah) offers pastries, a bar is similar to an American bar that serves drinks and appetizers, and a cantina is a lower-class drinking establishment that women usually do not frequent.

Japanese, Chinese, Italian, Spanish, Middle Eastern, or French restaurants are also found in urban areas. Many of these establishments

An outdoor café beckons both locals and tourists in the Casco Viejo historic district of Panama City.

are moderately priced, so it is common for Panamanians to dine out often. Panamanian manners dictate that the person who invites another to a restaurant or bar has to pay for the bill. In hotels and restaurants, it is customary to tip the staff 10 to 15 percent of the bill.

EATING HABITS

Panamanians eat three hearty meals per day—*el desayuno* (day-sigh-OO-noh), or breakfast, *el almuerzo* (ahl-MWER-soh), or lunch, and *la cena* (SAY-nah), or dinner. Typical breakfast fare consists of thick, deep-fried tortillas with a white cheese, sauteed liver, garlic, and onions, as well as fresh rolls or bread. Urban Panamanians sometimes have eggs to start their day too. Coffee is the most common breakfast beverage.

Unlike their neighbors, Panamanians do not consider lunch to be the main meal. A typical lunch begins with soup, followed by chicken or steak. Panamanians serve their meat with a mixture of cooked rice and red kidney beans, or pigeon peas. Salad is eaten with the main course.

The dinner meal usually consists of meat covered with a spicy sauce, rice, and salad. Panamanians love dessert, but it is usually fruit. Occasionally they indulge in cake, chocolate mousse, pie, or cheesecake. After dinner Panamanians may enjoy a cup of coffee, such as espresso.

FAVORITE FOODS AND REGIONAL DELICACIES

Panama's different regions have different types of cuisine, but most Panamanians enjoy eating food from all over their country. The food from every region is usually quite spicy.

Fish is a staple in the national diet. The most popular fish is *corvina* (kohr-VEE-nah), or sea bass. Panamanians and Latin Americans' favorite appetizer is ceviche. To prepare ceviche, Panamanians season raw sea bass with small yellow and red peppers, and thinly sliced onions. They marinate the mixture

A dish of ceviche is eaten cold.

overnight in lemon juice and serve it raw. Ceviche is not simply raw fish, however. The acid in the lemon juice "cooks" the flesh. Panamanians also use their favorite fish, sea bass, to make *bolitas de pescado* (boh-LEE-tahs day pes-CAH-doh), which are breaded and fried balls of fish meat. Although Panama's shrimp and lobster are also excellent, these regional delicacies are usually reserved for special occasions.

Another source of food are sea turtle eggs. Poor rural families

Meat-filled empanadas are a favorite dish.

eat the sea turtles' eggs for protein, and urban Panamanians view the eggs as a gourmet food. One turtle will lay as many as 150 eggs, which rural Panamanians collect and sell for less than a dollar each. Over the past few years, the turtle population has declined, so environmentalists are trying to save the eggs from human consumption.

One of Panamanians' favorite meat dishes is *ropa vieja* (ROH-pah bee-AY-hah). To prepare this dish, Panamanians mix shredded beef with green peppers, spices, plantains, and rice. Other favorites include empanadas, or fried meat pies, and *lomo relleno* (LOH-moh ray-YAY-noh), which is steak stuffed with spices and herbs.

Panama is also famous for its wonderful soups and stews. The traditional soup, *sancocho* (san-KOH-choh), is prepared with chicken, corn, plantains, yucca, coriander leaves, and potatoes. Panamanians also use beef and seafood in their stews. *Guacho* is an everyday stew that is unlike many other Panamanian stews because it is more watery. It contains a lot of different ingredients and provides a complete, nutritional meal on its own.

The green iguana is considered as both a delicacy and a staple part of the Panamanian diet. Often called "chicken of the trees," the iguana's meat

Arroz con cacao is a popular chocolate rice pudding dessert.

and eggs are used in many dishes. To prevent the iguanas from being hunted to extinction, farmers rear them in captivity by controlled reproduction and incubation, before releasing the iguanas back into the forests when they are between six and ten months old.

The most popular Panamanian dessert is *sopa borracha* (SOH-pah bohr-RAH-chah), which is pound cake topped with syrup, rum or brandy, cinnamon, raisins, and cloves. If the chef adds whipped cream to sopa borracha, it is called *sopa de gloria* (SOH-pah day GLO-ree-ah). Two delicious rice-based Panamanian desserts are *arroz con cacao* (ahr-ROHS kohn cah-CAH-oh), a chocolate rice pudding, and *resbaladera* (rays-bah-lah-THAY-rah), which is made from rice, milk, vanilla, sugar, and cinnamon.

TABLE MANNERS AND ETIQUETTE

The father always sits at the head of the table. If the family has guests, the guest of honor sits at the other end of the table. In middle- and upper-class homes, a maid serves the food. Individual plates and main platters of food are placed on the table, and diners help themselves to the food. At a formal dinner, however, the maid serves each person from the platters. Once the food is served, the host will invite everyone to begin eating by saying "*buen provecho*," which doesn't have an equivalent in English (it translates literally into "good benefit") but means much the same as "*bon appetit*."

Panamanians signal that they have finished a meal by placing their cutlery vertically and parallel to their plates. The spoon is used more than the fork or knife. Hands are kept above the table and conversation while eating revolves around casual everyday topics, such as sports and the weather.

ENTERTAINING AT HOME

Panamanians are open and informal with their guests, and hosts always serve their guests first. Guests are given the best of everything and sometimes even a parting gift. Instead of giving their host a gift when invited to dinner, guests are expected to invite them to dinner in return.

When Panamanians dine at another person's home, good manners dictate that they should eat everything on their plate. If they really dislike something, however, it is not considered rude to leave it on the plate. Host families serve alcoholic drinks to their guests before, during, and after a meal. Offers by guests to help set the table or wash up are viewed as criticisms of the host's hospitality.

Traditionally, Panamanians dress nicely for most meals, even if they are not expecting guests. They also wear formal clothes when visiting another person's home for a meal. The man would wear a dark suit with a tie, while the woman usually prefers to wear a dress.

INTERNET LINKS

www.hablayapanama.com/blog/2014/07/what-do-panamanians-eat-traditionally-typical-meals-in-panama
Many photos of traditional Panamanian dishes are featured on this site.

www.vacationtopanama.com/travel-guide/about-panama/cuisine
This travel site offers information on Panamanian foods, grocery stores, and some traditional recipes.

ARROZ CON POLLO (CHICKEN WITH RICE)

¼ cup (60 milliliters) vegetable oil

1 (4 to 6 pound) (1.8 to 2.7 kg) whole chicken, cut into pieces

1 onion, chopped

1 green bell pepper, chopped

2 cloves garlic, minced

1 (14.5 ounce) (400 g) can stewed tomatoes

1 cup (190 g) rice

¼ teaspoon saffron

2 teaspoon salt, or to taste

1 teaspoon dried oregano

½ teaspoon ground black pepper

1 bay leaf

2 cups (475 mL) chicken stock, or as needed to cover

1 cup (150 g) green peas, lightly cooked

½ cup (75 g) pimento-stuffed green olives, sliced

Preheat oven to 350°F (175°C).

Heat oil in a Dutch oven over medium heat; cook and stir chicken pieces until browned, 5 to 10 minutes. Add onion, green bell pepper, and garlic and cook until softened, about 5 minutes.

Add tomatoes, rice, saffron, salt, oregano, black pepper, and bay leaf. Pour in enough chicken stock to cover all the ingredients. Cover the pan and place in the oven.

Bake the chicken-rice mixture until rice is tender and chicken is no longer pink in the center and the juices run clear, about 1 hour and 30 minutes. Stir peas and olives into the chicken-rice mixture.

FLAN DE CARAMELO (CARAMEL CUSTARD)

1 cup (200 g) white sugar (for caramel)
3 large eggs
1 can (12 oz) (354 mL) evaporated milk
1 can (14 oz) (397 g) of sweetened condensed milk
1 tablespoon vanilla

Preheat oven to 350°F (175°C).

In a medium saucepan over medium-low heat, melt sugar, stirring constantly, for about 3 or 4 minutes or until liquefied and golden in color. (Watch carefully, sugar can burn quickly.)

Carefully pour hot syrup into a 9-inch round glass baking dish, turning the dish to evenly coat the bottom and sides. Set aside.

In a medium bowl, mix the milks, eggs, and vanilla, and pour into the caramel-lined baking dish. Cover the dish with aluminum foil.

Bake for about 1 hour. Remove, let it cool completely, and then place in the refrigerator.

To serve, carefully invert the dish onto a serving plate (with a rim to catch the liquid).

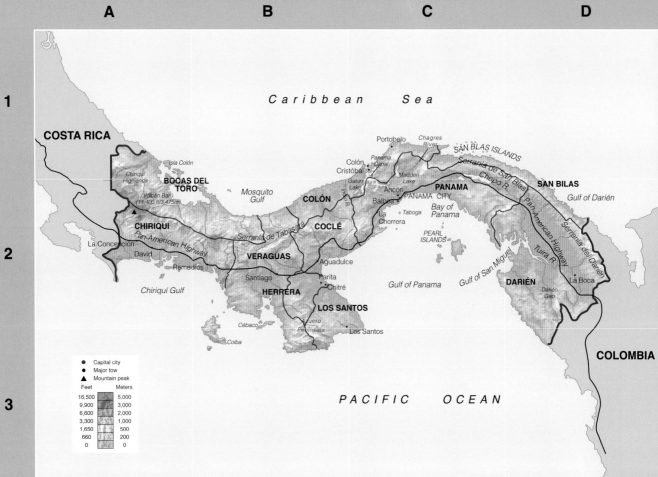

A   **B**   **C**   **D**

1

Caribbean   Sea

COSTA RICA

Isla Colón

*Chiriqui
Highlands*

**BOCAS DEL
TORO**

*Mosquito
Gulf*

Portobelo   *Chagres
River*

SAN BLAS ISLANDS

*Panama
Canal*

Colón

Cristóbal

COLÓN

Serrania de San Blas

Chepo R.

SAN BILAS

Gulf of Darién

*Volcán Barú
(11,400 ft/3,475m)*

*Gatun
Lake*

*Madden
Lake*

Ancón

PANAMA

CHIRIQUI

Balboa   **PANAMA CITY**

Serrania del Darién

Pan-American Highway

La
Chorrera

Taboga

*Bay of
Panama*

Pan-American Highway

2

La Concención

Serrania de Tabasará

COCLÉ

David

VERAGUAS

*PEARL
ISLANDS*

Tuira R.

Remedios

Aguadulce

Gulf of San Miguel

DARIÉN

La Boca

Chiriquí Gulf

Santiago

Parita

Gulf of Panama

*Darién
Gap*

Chitré

HERRERA

LOS SANTOS

Cébaco

*Azuero
Peninsula*

Los Santos

COLOMBIA

Coiba

● Capital city
● Major tow
▲ Mountain peak

Feet   Meters

16,500	5,000
9,900	3,000
6,600	2,000
3,300	1,000
1,650	500
660	200
0	0

3

PACIFIC   OCEAN

MAP OF PANAMA

ECONOMIC PANAMA

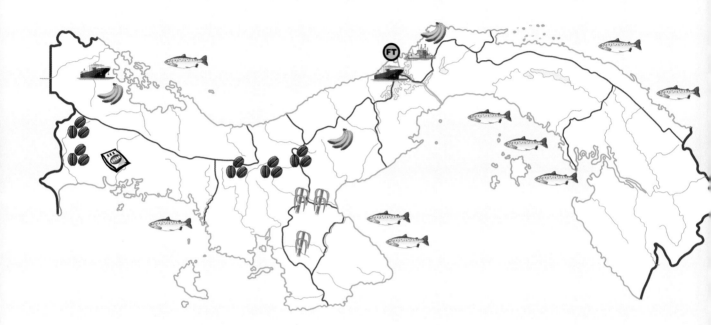

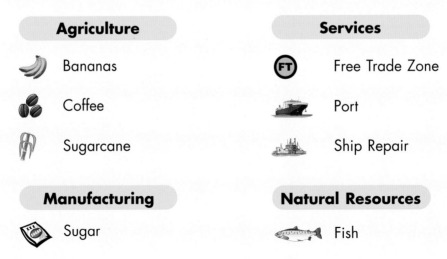

Agriculture

- Bananas
- Coffee
- Sugarcane

Manufacturing

- Sugar

Services

- FT Free Trade Zone
- Port
- Ship Repair

Natural Resources

- Fish

ABOUT THE ECONOMY

OVERVIEW
Panama's economy is bolstered largely by the revenue generated by the Panama Canal and the world's second largest duty-free port.

GROSS DOMESTIC PRODUCT (GDP)
$52.13 billion (2015 estimate)

GDP BY SECTOR
Services 77 percent, industry 20 percent, agriculture 3 percent (2015)

GDP PER CAPITA
$21,800 (2015)

LABOR FORCE
1.6 million (2015) (shortage of skilled labor, but an oversupply of unskilled labor)

LABOR FORCE BY SECTOR
Services 64.4 percent, industry 18.6 percent, agriculture 17 percent (2009)

UNEMPLOYMENT RATE
4.5 percent (2015)

POPULATION BELOW POVERTY LINE
26 percent (2012)

CURRENCY
The paper currency is the US dollar. The balboa is the coin currency.

1 balboa = 100 centesimos
USD 1 = 1 balboa (PAB) (2016)

NATURAL RESOURCES
Mahogany, copper, hydropower, seafood

AGRICULTURAL PRODUCTS
Bananas, rice, corn, sugar, coffee, sugarcane, vegetables, livestock, shrimp

INDUSTRY AND MANUFACTURING
Construction, brewing, cement and other construction materials, sugar milling

IMPORTS
fuels, machinery, vehicles, iron and steel rods, pharmaceuticals

EXPORTS
Fruit and nuts, fish, iron and steel waste, wood

IMPORT PARTNERS
United States 25.9 percent, China 9.6 percent, Mexico 5.1 percent (2015)

MAJOR EXPORT MARKETS
United States 19.7 percent, Germany 13.2 percent, Costa Rica 7.7 percent, China 5.9 percent, Netherlands 4.1 percent (2015)

CULTURAL PANAMA

Parque Nacional Volcán Barú
Parque Nacional Volcán Barú covers more than 34,594 acres (14,000 ha) and provides walking trails, hiking routes, mountain climbing activities, and camping sites.

Panamá la Vieja
Founded nearly five hundred years ago, Panamá la Vieja was the first European city on the Pacific coast of the Americas.

Church of the Black Christ
Church of the Black Christ is located in Portobelo. A festival is held in its honor annually.

Catedral de Nuestra Señora de la Asunción
Catedral de Nuestra Señora de la Asunción and its bell tower were built between 1619 and 1626.

Casa Alarcón
Casa Alarcón, also known as Casa del Obispo (Bishop's House), was a three-story house where the bishop used to reside.

The Corredor Sur
The Corredor Sur arches also make for a stunning sight at night, when the ruins are illuminated.

Volcán Barú
Volcán Barú measures about 11,400 feet (3,475 m) high and has seven craters.

Plaza de la Independencia
This is where Panama's independence was declared.

Casco Viejo
Founded in 1673, Casco Viejo, commonly known as Casco Antiguoor San Felipe, was declared a World Heritage Site by UNESCO in 1997.

Iglesia de San José
It is also known as the Church of the Golden Altar.

Comarca de Kuna Yala
Comarca de Kuna Yala encompasses the 365 islands of Archipiélago de San Blas. It is home to the Gunas who have governed the region since the 1920s, with minimal interference from the national government.

ABOUT THE CULTURE

FLAG
Adopted in 1904, the Panamanian flag is divided into four equal rectangles. The top-left and bottom-right rectangles are white, with a blue and a red star respectively in the middle, while the top-right and bottom-left rectangles are red and blue respectively. Red and blue represent the Liberal and Conservative parties, the two main political parties at the time of Panama's independence. White symbolizes peace between the two parties.

OFFICIAL NAME
Republic of Panama

CAPITAL
Panama City

INDEPENDENCE
November 3, 1903 (from Colombia)
November 28, 1821 (from Spain)

POPULATION
3.7 million (2015 estimate)

LIFE EXPECTANCY
Male 75.7 years, female 81.4 years (2015)

ETHNIC GROUPS
Mestizo 65 percent, Native American 12.3 percent, Afro-Caribbean 9.2 percent, mulatto, 6.8 percent, Caucasian 6.7 percent

LANGUAGES
Spanish (official), English, nine indigenous languages. Most Panamanians are bilingual.

LITERACY RATE
95 percent (2015)

RELIGIOUS GROUPS
Roman Catholic 85 percent, Protestant 15 percent

MAJOR CITIES
Panama City, Colón, David, Santiago

PROVINCES
Bocas del Toro, Chiriquí, Veraguas, Colón, Coclé, Herrera, Los Santos, Panama, Darién

INDIGENOUS TERRITORIES
Guna Yala, Emberá, Madungandí, Ngöbe-Buglé

TIMELINE

IN PANAMA	IN THE WORLD
	753 BCE Rome is founded.
	116–117 BCE The Roman Empire reaches its greatest extent, under Emperor Trajan.
	600 CE Height of Mayan civilization
1502 Spanish explorer Rodrigo de Bastidas visits Panama, which was home to Cuna, Choco, Guaymi, and other indigenous peoples.	**1000** The Chinese perfect gunpowder and begin to use it in warfare.
1519 Pedro Arias de Ávila (or Pedrarias the Cruel) establishes the city of Panama.	**1530** Beginning of transatlantic slave trade organized by the Portuguese in Africa
	1558–1603 Reign of Elizabeth I of England
1671 Henry Morgan overpowers Fuerte San Lorenzo, then sacks the city of Panama; a new walled city is later built a few miles away.	**1620** Pilgrims sail the *Mayflower* to America.
	1776 US Declaration of Independence
	1789–1799 The French Revolution
1830 Panama becomes part of Colombia following the collapse of Gran Colombia.	**1861** The US Civil War begins.
	1869 The Suez Canal is opened.
1914 The Panama Canal is completed.	**1914–1917** World War I
	1939–1945 World War II
	1949 The North Atlantic Treaty Organization (NATO) is formed.
	1957 The Russians launch *Sputnik*.

IN PANAMA	IN THE WORLD
	1966–1969 The Chinese Cultural Revolution
1968–1981 General Omar Torrijos Herrera overthrows elected president Arnulfo Arias and imposes a dictatorship.	
1983 Former intelligence chief and Central Intelligence Agency operative Manuel Noriega becomes military dictator of Panama.	**1986** Nuclear power disaster at Chernobyl in Ukraine
1989 US invasion of Panama, Noriega is captured and flown to the United States.	**1991** Breakup of the Soviet Union **1997** Hong Kong is returned to China.
1999 Mireya Moscoso becomes Panama's first woman president; the United States hands the canal over to Panama and withdraws all its military bases in the country, ending nearly 100 years of US administration over the canal.	**2001** Terrorists crash planes in New York, Washington DC, and Pennsylvania. **2003** War in Iraq begins.
2004 Martín Torrijos wins the presidential elections.	
2006 Panamanians support referendum to expand the Panama Canal.	
2007 Noriega's US prison sentence ends; he is extradited to France to be retried for murder and money laundering.	**2008** US elects first African-American president Barack Obama.
2009 Ricardo Martinelli wins presidential election.	
2011 Noriega is extradited from France to Panama to serve twenty-year sentence there.	
2016 The newly expanded Panama Canal opens to ship traffic. Government of Panama launches investigation into 1989 US invasion.	**2015–2016** ISIS sympathizers launch terror attacks in Belgium and France.

GLOSSARY

audiencia (ow-dee-EHN-see-ah)
Spanish court; the basic administrative unit for Spain's American colonies.

chivas (CHEE-vahs)
Buses with brightly painted panels.

comparsas (cohm-PAHR-sahs)
Groups of people celebrating.

cordillera (korh-dee-YAIR-ah)
Mountain chain.

corvina (kohr-VEE-nah)
Sea bass.

cumbia (KOOM-byah)
Popular Panamanian dance.

fiesta (fee-AYS-tah)
Festival or party.

guro (GOO-roh)
Ngöbe-Buglé ritual for young men.

inna-nega (een-NAH nay-GAH)
Guna celebration for young women.

kantule (kahn-TOO-lay)
Guna priest.

mejorana (may-hoh-RAH-na)
Traditional Panamanian folk song.

mestizos (may-STEE-zos)
People of mixed Indian and Spanish descent.

mola (MOH-lah)
Guna embroidered cloth.

montuno (mohn-TOO-noh)
National clothing for Panamanian men.

peineta (peh-ee-NEH-tah)
Headpiece worn with the *pollera*.

pintado (pin-TAH-doh)
Straw hat worn by men with the national clothing.

pollera (poh-YEH-rah)
National dress for Panamanian women: a long, full dress of white cotton with brightly colored embroidery.

salsa
Music that is a blend of rock, jazz, and rhythm and blues with Cuban rhythms.

tamborito (tahm-boh-REE-toh)
Panamanian national dance.

FOR FURTHER INFORMATION

BOOKS

Friar, William. *Portrait of the Panama Canal: Celebrating Its History and Expansion*. Portland, OR: Graphic Arts Books, 2016

Lindsay-Poland, John. *Emperors in the Jungle: The Hidden History of the U.S. in Panama*. Durham, NC: Duke University Press, 2003.

Lonely Planet, and Carolyn McCarthy. *Lonely Planet Panama*. Oakland, CA: Lonely Planet, 2013.

McCullough, David. *The Path Between the Seas: The Creation of Panama Canal, 1870–1914*. New York: Simon & Schuster, 1978.

ONLINE

American Experience. *Panama Canal*. www.pbs.org/wgbh/americanexperience/films/panama

Canal de Panamá. www.pancanal.com/eng

CIA World Factbook. Panama. www.cia.gov/library/publications/the-world-factbook/geos/pm.html

History. Panama Canal. www.history.com/topics/panama-canal

The Huffington Post. "A Man, a Plan, a Canal—Panama." www.huffingtonpost.com/laura-grier/a-man-a-plan-a-canal-panama_b_6966942.html

Lonely Planet. Panama. www.lonelyplanet.com/panama

The New York Times, Panama news and archives. www.nytimes.com/topic/destination/panama

FILMS

American Experience: Panama Canal. PBS, 2011. DVD.

NOVA: A Man, a Plan, a Canal, Panama. PBS, 2004, DVD.

BIBLIOGRAPHY

Anywhere Panama. http://www.anywherepanama.com.

Canal de Panamá. https://www.pancanal.com/eng.

CIA World Factbook. Panama. https://www.cia.gov/library/publications/the-world-factbook/geos/pm.html.

Lonely Planet. Panama. https://www.lonelyplanet.com/panama.

New York Times, The. Panama news and archives. www.nytimes.com/topic/destination/panama.

Pew Research Center. "Religion in Latin America." November 13, 2014. http://www.pewforum.org/2014/11/13/religion-in-latin-america.

Power Engineering International. "Panama pushes forward with hydropower plan." http://www.powerengineeringint.com/articles/2016/02/panama-pushes-forward-with-hydropower-plan.html.

Smith, Roff. "A Hundred Years Old Today, the Panama Canal Is About to Get a Lot Bigger." *National Geographic*, August 16, 2014. http://news.nationalgeographic.com/news/2014/08/140815-panama-canal-culebra-cut-lake-gatun-focus.

INDEX

INDEX